Allan Menzies

National religion

Sermons on the Ten Commandments

Allan Menzies

National religion
Sermons on the Ten Commandments

ISBN/EAN: 9783337264857

Printed in Europe, USA, Canada, Australia, Japan

Cover: Foto ©Lupo / pixelio.de

More available books at **www.hansebooks.com**

NATIONAL RELIGION.

NATIONAL RELIGION:

SERMONS

ON

THE TEN COMMANDMENTS.

BY

REV. ALLAN MENZIES,

Abernyte.

ALEXANDER GARDNER,
PAISLEY; AND 12 PATERNOSTER ROW, LONDON.

1888.

CONTENTS.

	PAGE.
PREFACE,	7
I.—THE LAW WAS GIVEN BY MOSES,	9
II.—THE LAW WRITTEN ON THE HEART,	26
III.—THE FIRST COMMANDMENT,	42
IV.—THE SECOND COMMANDMENT,	60
V.—THE THIRD COMMANDMENT,	75
VI.—THE FOURTH COMMANDMENT,	89
VII.—THE FIFTH COMMANDMENT, I.,	107
VIII.—THE FIFTH COMMANDMENT, II.,	121
IX.—THE SIXTH COMMANDMENT,	132
X.—THE SEVENTH COMMANDMENT,	146
XI.—THE EIGHTH COMMANDMENT,	159
XII.—THE NINTH COMMANDMENT,	172
XIII.—THE TENTH COMMANDMENT,	184

PREFACE.

Some of these sermons are printed substantially as they were preached to my congregation at Abernyte; some of them have received considerable additions, and might almost be called studies rather than sermons. One, that on the seventh commandment, has been written for this volume.

It appears to me that the church is specially called in present circumstances, to the defence on religious grounds of the foundations of society, and that even a fragmentary attempt to shew that the various arrangements of the social state have their basis in reason and necessity, or in other words, the will of God, may not be without its use.

It will be found by those who consider the matter without prejudice, that the Decalogue gains instead of losing in impressiveness, when the verdict of criticism is frankly accepted, which assigns it in its present form to the age of the prophets. In the writings of these great men we can read the record of the sorrowful experience, which called for the promulgation of such a code.

The Ten Commandments.

I.

The law was given by Moses.

"There he made for them a statute and an ordinance, and there he proved them."—Exodus xv. 25.

THE Decalogue, or the Law of the Ten Words or Ten Commandments, is the code of laws which we all know best. But our very familiarity with these great precepts may possibly have prevented us from thinking of their meaning as much as we should; and it is proposed to devote a series of discourses to the consideration of them. How were these commandments called for, we shall ask, and what did they mean to those who first heard them? If we can see how they were at first found necessary we shall no doubt understand more clearly what they mean as applied to ourselves.

In this discourse we shall seek to give a short historical introduction to the Decalogue. In what way was it given, we shall ask; how did it come to be what it is? Most laws are the result of long experience, often of painful experience; law does not come first in man's existence on this earth, but a state without law: and laws are given to enable men to escape from the evils of that state, and to establish their social life on a firm basis. Is the Decalogue an exception to this rule, or not? Were these laws all dictated entire out of heaven, or were they like other laws, the result of a long process of growth in civilisation? Did they come into the world all at once as a complete code, and were they imposed on men by an external, supramundane authority, on a certain day, or had each of them a growth of its own, and are some of them, possibly, earlier than others?

The Decalogue is inseparably connected with the name of Moses, and the best way of approaching an answer to the questions we have asked, may be to enquire as to the character of Moses' work as a legislator. Let us take before us not only the story of Sinai, which is of a symbolical dramatic nature, but what we know generally of Moses' aims and procedure, and see what we can learn, starting from this point, as to the origin of the Ten Commandments.

Before Moses, Israel had no laws, at least no system, no code of law: Israel, in fact, had no unity, and had not yet become a nation. The tribes whom Moses led out of Egypt could scarcely be called a nation: they were merely certain tribes of bondsmen loosely connected with each other by common memories of a dim past, in which their ancestors were free; but the tie was still wanting which might hold them permanently together. We justly regard it as the greatest act of Moses, that he led the children of Israel out of Egypt. Fired with the instinct of a liberator, he summoned his people in the name of their ancestral deity, to shake off their degradation. When they arose at his call and marched away from their taskmasters, he led them farther than they expected: in the most mysterious and astonishing way, he led them across an arm of the sea to a country where the voice of their oppressors could not reach them. Almost without any exertions of their own they passed from bondage to liberty; Moses in God's name delivered them from the pots and broke the yoke from off their shoulders.

But it still remained to be seen whether they were capable of freedom. Were they fit to hold together, was there a spirit in them which would lead them to pursue a common object, and to stand up in the world as a separate nationality, instead of melting away in the surrounding peoples? If they did not possess this capacity, then the work of emancipating them could lead to no result. Had this people which now stood on the shore of the desert in the enjoyment of liberty and with the open world before them, proved incapable of organised national life, the Exodus would never have been heard of.

It was the second part of the work of Moses to provide the people he had set free with the basis of their civil life. The work of liberation was only half of what he did for them. He also convinced them of the object for which that liberation had been accomplished, and which they never wholly ceased in all their subsequent history to keep in view, and he taught them how to live together as a people.

This work of moulding them into a nation could not be accomplished in a day. The Exodus itself was hurriedly gone about, and was an accomplished fact before the enthusiasm which led to it had time to cool, but the settling of the habits and the forming of the spirit of the newborn nation must from the nature of the case have been a work of time. The excitement of the Exodus is followed by the forty years in the wilderness. But these forty years were not lost. They were the seed time of the history of Israel.

Our text speaks of a place where God proved or made trial of the people, and where he also gave them a statute and an ordinance, laws and observances to keep. The two things are closely connected with each other. The people were proved by the statute and the ordinance which were laid upon them. The verse stands before the history of the visit to Sinai, but the opinion is held by some scholars that it refers to the period after that event; and that the place it speaks of is Kadesh, where the Israelites abode many days during their wanderings, where Moses smote the rock which gave the people water, where Miriam died, and from whence the spies were sent out to view the promised land. The verse certainly applies very well to the time of the moulding of the tribes into a nation. Restraints were then imposed on them different from the restraints of slavery under which they had been brought up, namely those of law and order, which are suitable and necessary for a free people. It thus came to be seen in the language of the Bible, whether they would keep the commandments of the Lord or not, or in our own language, whether they were capable of discipline and common action, and therefore fit for a national existence. During these forty years the Israelites were being trained to the habits and observances without which no nation can maintain itself, or do any useful work in the world. The laws were being given to them which, in all subsequent periods of their history, they were to regard as sacred and fundamental. The foundations of their national conscience were being laid. The tendency was being impressed upon them which their national development was to follow, and in fact did follow in after times. Thus Moses was justly regarded afterwards not only as the great liberator who saved his people from the bondage of Egypt, but also as the great legislator, at whose hands they had received the divine laws under which they lived. The law was given by Moses, and the law was the spirit of Israel. It may be questioned if any other man has been the author of a work so fruitful of happy and far-reaching influence for mankind, as that of Moses in laying the foundation of the Jewish state. If, as is unquestionable, the Jews have contributed more to the elevation and salvation of the world than any other race, and if it was Moses who made them a nation and started them on their career by the laws he gave them, it is impossible to exaggerate his historical importance, or to pay too great honour to his name.

But what laws did Moses give? Old Testament scholars tell us that very little of the abundant mass of legislation in the Pentateuch can be ascribed to him, because even if he were to some extent a man of letters (and it is doubtful if he could be so), any written words of his which survive must be extremely short. And when we remember the manner in which Moses dispensed justice to the people, we see that he gave them laws not principally by writing them down but in another way. In the eighteenth chapter of Exodus, we read how, at one period—the period, probably, spoken of in the text, when Israel sojourned at Kadesh—many cases were brought to him for decision, so many, in fact, as to take up nearly his whole time. This was his law-giving: his laws were like those of the early legislators of other peoples, decisions or "dooms" ($\theta\acute{\epsilon}\mu\iota\sigma\tau\alpha s$) which, passing into general knowledge, acquired the force of customary law. He gave his people statutes and ordinances by discharging among them the office of a judge; his sentences were no doubt founded on the floating system of law already known to them, and served in their turn afterwards to build up the national system. His law was case-law, and known afterwards only by the result to which it had contributed.

But was this the only way in which Moses gave laws to Israel? Did he give no written laws?

Was he not the author of the religious and civil constitution under which the people lived? It has been commonly believed among us that the whole Pentateuch was the work of Moses: are we to end with the belief that it contains none of his work at all?

As for laws which Moses may have written, we have to recognize that criticism demands quite clearly, and with practical unanimity, that we should cease to regard as belonging to him any of the legislation which deals with ritual. The Book of Deuteronomy, we are told, belongs to the reformation of Josiah. The specifications about the tabernacle, the priests, the sacrifices, the sacred seasons, belong to the period after the captivity. The editing of the Pentateuch, as we have it, is due to some successor of Ezra. Moses was regarded as the great law-giver, and all laws which God was considered to have sanctioned were placed under his name, that being the regular and only method of conferring authority upon new enactments. It might therefore appear that no laws at all are left, of which Moses can be regarded as the immediate author.

But criticism, which takes so much away from Moses, does not take all. It recognises that the precepts of the Decalogue are such as one in Moses' position may reasonably be supposed to have promulgated. The central notion of the Decalogue, which is to invest the natural laws of social life with a religious sanction, is acknowledged to be in the true spirit of Moses. The ten commandments, therefore, may be regarded as his, in spirit at least, if not altogether in form.

As to the present form of the Decalogue, various considerations point to a later age than that of Moses. Some of the precepts now contained in it he can scarcely be believed to have given; some of them he may have given, but not precisely as we have them. The considerations which point to this conclusion may be briefly enumerated.

If Moses was the author of a Decalogue or law of ten commandments, scholars are agreed that these commandments must have been quite short, and have consisted of peremptory injunctions, such as the sixth, seventh, and eighth are; any stones which could be carried about in the ark would contain very little writing. The ten commandments of Moses would in fact be a law of ten words; this is what the name Decalogue indicates. Accordingly the long reasons annexed to some of the commandments can scarcely belong to the period of the wanderings. Again, it is well known that the Bible contains two versions of the Decalogue, one in Exodus xx., the other in Deuteronomy v., and that these two versions differ from each other in important particulars. The parts which differ can scarcely proceed from the same author, and it is natural to suppose that those portions in which the variations occur do not belong to the original, but were added to it by later writers. Again, the xxxivth chapter of Exodus gives a law of ten commandments, said to have been written by Moses, at the direction of God, on two tables of stone; but these laws, which are said to embody the covenant of Jehovah with Israel, are entirely different from the Decalogue of Exodus xx. In these laws God prescribes the kind of sacrifice which it is right to offer him; they embody the primitive ideas on which the early cultus of the Jews was formed. But Moses put the claims of justice and mercy before those of sacrifice; the whole history of the Jewish religion is unintelligible if he did not rise to this higher conception of the divine will. The Book of Exodus contains two Decalogues, thus showing that the notion of formulating the requirements of God in ten compendious precepts, existed from early times, and was applied in various ways. But we may be sure that the Decalogue accepted by the Jewish Church represents most faithfully the spirit of Moses.

While however the spirit of these ten words may be accepted as the spirit of Moses, there are reasons for doubting whether the laws taken individually can all be regarded as his work. The broad and universal tone of the Decalogue is thought by some scholars to belong to a more advanced age than that of Sinai; if Moses framed a compendium of the Divine will in ten words, must not these words, it is asked, have been of a somewhat more national character, somewhat less broadly human and cosmopolitan than those now before us? Some of the commandments must have been in force before Moses, as they embody the essential conditions of all social life. Some of them cannot have reached general recognition till long after him, as they presuppose quite a different state of society from that existing in his day; and Moses could scarcely be the author of a law which the social arrangements of his day afforded no opportunities of observing. The fifth commandment assigns a position to woman as head of the house along with her husband, which it may be doubted if she had attained in the age of Moses. The fourth and the tenth commandments are addressed to an agricultural population, to people living on farms and having servants under them: but the Israelites with whom Moses had to deal were not farmers but wanderers in the desert, who drove their flocks and herds from pasture to pasture. And the second commandment, which forbids the use of images, could scarcely be by Moses, who himself made an image of a serpent which was worshipped by his fellow-countrymen down to the days of Hezekiah. The Israelites in the days of the Judges saw nothing shocking in the worship of images; and we know that Jehovah was worshipped even in the time of Elijah under the form of a bull, without any feeling on the part of the worshippers, or even to all appearances on the part of the great prophet, that it was contrary to the genius of the national religion to do so.

Considering these points and others of a like nature, the leading students of the Old Testament history are inclined to hold that if Moses gave a law of ten words, some of them at least must have been different from those which we now have. The Decalogue as we have it, does not reflect the standard of conduct which prevailed in his day or for a long time after him; it reflects, indeed, a standard of conduct which only became fully present to the Jewish mind many centuries later, under the influence of the prophets. It may be said that in the enthusiasm of the period of the Exodus, the faith of Moses and of the people might lay hold of a much higher and more advanced ideal than could at that time be permanently maintained; so that the Decalogue might be regarded as an early anticipation of a state of things not yet established, of views and convictions which Israel was destined to reach in the course of its moral growth, or as a promise not then nor for many centuries afterwards fulfilled. But surely we must think that laws like these, if once they had appeared in their majestic authority to the mind of Israel, could not have left so little trace upon the views of the people as some of the commandments must have done if Moses promulgated them; and it appears on the whole safer and more reverent to conclude that there are some of the ten commandments which Moses probably never gave, and which were only set up as Divine laws at a period long after him.

What then did Moses do? What was his work as a legislator? In what way did the law come by him?

He wrote no works that we can read, but he was the founder of the Jewish religion. He brought the people of Israel to adopt as their own the best of all the gods, and after the events of the exodus he set up the covenant between the people and the God who had delivered them, a covenant which, however often they broke it, they were never able to forget, and which in later centuries laid hold of their consciences with growing power.

The never-to-be-forgotten service Moses rendered to mankind was that he declared, and caused his people to believe, that their God, who, as we now remember, was destined to be supreme not in the Jewish nation only, but in the most enlightened and powerful nations of the world at a later time, was a righteous God, and that justice and righteousness were what he required first of all from men. The words which he set before his people as the expression of the divine will were not about any mysterious and recondite affairs, they were not about sacrifice and offering; they dealt with those plain duties which a man's conscience tells him that he owes to God and to his fellow-creatures. The morality of Moses' day may have been in some respects rudimentary, and to our minds defective, but such morality as man's mind had then compassed Moses set up as the law of God for him. Your God whom you cannot see, he said, is just and righteous; that is the first thing to be said about him; and it is by being just and righteous that you can best please him.

Thus Moses set up the great principle that the true sphere of religion is common life. The duties we owe to each other, those duties which conscience requires us to do, and by doing which alone we can gain the confidence of others, and live at peace with them in society, those duties which the interests of the human race imperatively command us not to scorn nor to forget, Moses declared to be what God's chief laws enjoin. This was a truth which Israel never forgot, and which in the age of the prophets was clothed in an immortal form in the law of the ten commandments.

II.

The Law written in the Heart.

Exodus xx. 1.—" God spake all these words."

THE Bible tells us that the ten commandments, which declare to us the fundamental duties which we owe to God and to our fellow-men, were spoken from heaven by God himself to his own people who were assembled, trembling and awe-struck, to receive them. They are thus invested with all the weight and impressiveness that religion can lend them. The Israelites have come from a land where there were visible gods in abundance, to worship a God whom no human eye can behold; and after travelling over a laborious road they have at length reached the spot where the invisible deliverer, who opened a path for them through the midst of the sea, is to be formally introduced to them as their God. In the midst of the most desolate scenery, and looking up to the great mountain where he has his seat, they await his voice. Everything is done to impress them with the awfulness of the occasion; they are bidden to prepare themselves most specially several days beforehand for the momentous interview; they are warned not to touch the mountain, on the penalty of death; the approach of the Most High is heralded by a great storm of thunder and lightning. After all this preparation and expectation he at length speaks to them, and makes known to them his will; and these commandments are the words he speaks; he requires of them nothing but the simplest duties, the first works, of religion and morality.

Now the laws which the Book of Exodus represents as having been published to the Israelites with such overwhelming pomp and circumstance, are laws which men have come to know in many other ways. These elementary duties which man owes to God and to his fellow-creatures have been revealed to him at sundry times and in divers manners. They have been taught not to one nation only, but to every nation that ever prospered in the world; and men have learned them by slow degrees and through painful experience. No people has a monopoly of them: they are indeed so plain and natural when once discovered, that we regard them as laws for all mankind, universal precepts which must be binding upon all, and which the conscience of all men is formed to recognise.

These fundamental laws were known to older peoples than Israel. The Egyptians knew them long before the Israelites left Egypt or came there. In the Book of the Dead, which instructed the Egyptian how to prepare himself for his last judgment, he was taught that in that important day he must be able to say, among other things, that he had not told lies nor committed murder, that he had not committed adultery, that he had blasphemed neither God nor his father, that he had not mocked God nor despised God in his heart. If the Decalogue had been published in Egypt, it would not perhaps have appeared to announce anything new. The Chinese had a body of admirable moral precepts, of a cold sensible kind, long before Moses. And a morality more closely bound up with religion was preached in India at a very early time.

Indeed, no country could be civilised or could make any figure in the world in which these laws were not known and respected. Men must have been learning them by experience from the first, all over the world. To see how these laws first made their appearance among men, we should require to go back beyond all written history, for there could be no community with any history to write till they had at least to some extent prevailed. Those who have made the early stages of human life upon the globe their study, could tell us something of the story. The uncurbed indulgence of cupidity, lust, and anger, they would tell us, was seen very early to be fatal to man's aspirations after security and progress, and the time when the community began to impose moral restraints upon its members, is one of which we cannot hope to know anything save by conjecture. Wherever in the wide world man has risen to a settled and orderly life, these fundamental laws are reverenced; often, it is true, along with a number of others of an arbitrary and fanciful nature. Wherever man has formed a community, there impiety, murder, adultery, and theft, have been publicly forbidden. These laws have at all times, indeed, been liable to be broken, they are often broken still, but society upholds them and defends itself against those who set them at naught, and in our own system of justice we see that defence of them by society against individual lawlessness, which has been going on from the beginning. The man of violence and fraud is more and more regarded as a public enemy, the breaches of the moral law are visited with public condemnation and with punishment, and are thus made the means of impressing that law more firmly on men's minds.

The legislation of Sinai accordingly was not the publication of a new law, but the publication of a law which was as old as man himself. The book of Exodus compresses into a great dramatic act a legislative work which was nowhere accomplished at one point of time, but was carried on in every land gradually, through a course of centuries. And one reason why man thus discovered the moral law in the course of his history was that it was written from the beginning on his own heart, and that it is a part of his own nature.

The Bible itself implies in many ways that the moral law was not peculiar to Israel, but common to the human race. It represents the whole human race as descended from the same stock, and therefore partaking of the same nature, and it tells us that Adam ate of the tree of the knowledge of good and evil and thus entered on his moral education, even in the garden of Eden. The theory used to be largely held that a primitive revelation of the moral law was made by God to man before the dispersion of the human race, and carried by each of the scattered families to its future home. The Bible would lead us to adopt a simpler explanation of the universal diffusion of that law, and to believe that the moral nature with which God endowed man at the beginning was itself his teacher. The apostle Paul says that the heathen nations, though they have not the law which was given to the Jews, yet do by nature the works of the law, and thus show the work of the law to be written in their hearts. The law is given to man not only in the way of outward precept; the outward precept avails and is recognised as valid because the law is already present in the conscience. The universal obligations of morality are at once accepted by all, in proportion as they are understood. There are no sons of Adam who are not thus instructed in the way of righteousness; there is no race of men whom their own nature, if placed in favourable circumstances, does not teach that irreverence, fraud, murder, and unchastity, are things to be condemned and put away. The lesson may come slowly: superstition may for ages hinder its acceptance by setting up unnatural standards of goodness and insisting on sacrifice to the neglect of justice and mercy; but there is a conscience in all men which, even in the face of such obstructions, will teach them by degrees their duty towards the world above them and the world around them. The law was given to man at his creation; it is a part of his own reasonable nature.

Now if these things are so,—if the laws contained in the decalogue are such as men had arrived at in various lands long before Moses, if they are laws which every community insists on, and which reason and conscience of themselves enforce, what does it mean to say that God spake all these words? They have become known to man in a number of ways, and had the Decalogue never been published, we should not be ignorant of their obligation. Does it change their nature, does it add anything to their force, to say that God uttered them?

That way of speaking, we may observe in the first place, brings them home most directly and powerfully to the mind of a people, and renders them more effective than they could be made in any other garb. To men of unformed minds and undisciplined impulses, such as those whom the compilers of the decalogue were seeking to influence, it was not enough to discourse on the lessons of history or to appeal to the experience of other lands or to point to the testimony of conscience. All this the Hebrew prophets did; but these efforts needed condensation, if they were to check the impulses of violent men. A brief and simple rule of conduct is needed by all men, and when the problem is to check the movements of unruly desire among a people, no rule of a different character will serve. To say that God speaks thus and thus is to use language which every one understands, and which conveys a powerful impression to every mind. Gathered up into a divine law all the considerations which enforce morality are focussed in one direct and powerful ray upon the conscience, and transformed from cold lessons of experience or maxims of prudence into energetic rules of conduct in the mind of each individual. The invisible legislator has access to the mind even when the man is alone and even when he has closed his ears to the voice of society. The law is obeyed not because the interests of society require obedience, nor because public opinion asks for it, but in deference to a higher will than any on earth. To every one who needs the countenance of heavenly powers, to every one who has sins to be forgiven or sorrows to be comforted, and there are few who are not included in these classes of men, the moral law is spoken when he lifts his eyes on high, and the observance of it is made the condition of the blessing which he craves. It is difficult to overestimate the service which religion renders to society when it puts in the forefront of its requirements the keeping of those laws which are the essential conditions of order and freedom. It is a matter of infinite value to the state to be supported by a power which calls the citizens by higher sanctions than any which the state commands, to reverence the laws on which society is based.

The promulgation of these laws as divine has thus given them a force they could not otherwise have obtained, and has been a great blessing to the world: but is it certain that they are divine? The statement that these words were spoken direct out of heaven by God on a particular day and at a particular spot on the earth's surface is clearly not a statement of a fact of history, but a dramatic way of putting a great lesson which is to be enforced. To many it may be useful to represent that lesson in a way in which it appeals to their imagination so directly and so powerfully, but it would be coming far short of the reasonable religion the commandments themselves enjoin, if we based the obligation of the Decalogue on the literal truth of the story of the twentieth chapter of Exodus. The laws were binding before the scene of Sinai, and are binding on those who never heard of that scene. But should it appear that some of these laws are much older than Moses and some of them much later, there are other grounds on which the assertion of the text that God spake all these words, can be maintained.

We have already noticed some of the ways in which the fundamental laws of morality have gathered their authority, quite apart from Moses. They have acquired it (1) by the experience of the human race. The progress of mankind from barbarism to civilization has proceeded in every part of the world on the same broad lines, and has everywhere consisted just in the gradual recognition and establishment of these laws. Barbarism may be defined as the state in which men are not governed by reasonable principles so much as by their needs and passions. Civilisation does not consist primarily or chiefly in stone houses and cultivated fields; it does not now consist principally in newspapers and machinery. It consists, first of all, in the tempers and habits which render those improvements possible; it is at hand when men have learned to respect one another's rights, and to be guided rather by invisible than by outward forces. Man has been learning everywhere that he could only rise by keeping certain laws. Every attempt to set these laws at naught leads in the individual to failure and ruin, and if on a large scale to national retrogression and disaster. In some parts of the world not far away, these lessons are not learned yet, but the world as a whole has learned to see in the fundamental laws the essential conditions of prosperity both for states and for individuals. These are the laws of all states: they are established by the universal consent of mankind.

(2) They are established no less distinctly by reason. When we turn our thoughts upon ourselves and consider what we are called to be to our fellowmen as members of society, we find that certain principles rise up before our minds which, apart from experience, we see it is necessary that we should respect in our intercourse with each other. There is no need to have gone about among many men or to have witnessed experiments of various kinds of conduct, in order to be

convinced of the necessity of these principles. Those who are childless and unwedded can draw out of their own minds correct views of the duties of married persons to each other and of the discipline which is necessary for the family; and a slave can delineate the virtues which can only be practised by freemen. And those laws with which we form acquaintance in our own breast we do not hesitate to apply to the conduct of those of whom we have no personal knowledge, and whose circumstances are widely different from ours. The fundamental rules of human conduct are not, we are assured, a matter of climate or of race; they are good for all men. We did not make them; we only discovered them, or, when they were stated to us, recognised at once their unquestionable force; we are sure that they are universally true; judging from the testimony of our own minds we conclude that they were there before there were any human minds to know them, that they were not made by man, and are beyond man's power to set aside or qualify.

Who imprinted on man's nature these great laws, and fixed it from the first that no state should flourish and no individual be happy without observing them? It is at once the simplest and the truest answer to such an enquiry to say that these laws were given to man by his Creator. Had he not been made for them from the first, they would in vain have been presented to him afterwards from without, they could never have acquired any real authority for him. Certainly it is the case that the moral ideas of early times differed widely from those now prevalent. They were occupied in many respects with other objects, they were enforced by different means, they contained much less of the element of reason. But the distinction between right and wrong, and the feelings of exaltation connected with doing right, of degradation connected with doing wrong, have always been an essential part of man's nature, and have driven him forward more powerfully than anything else on the path of progress. As he has grown stronger his conscience has grown more tender, he has found out new duties, morality has penetrated more into all the parts of his life, and has set before him higher ideals. The moral law has always been in course of disclosing itself, and is not fully published yet. And if it be the case that works which have taken measureless ages to accomplish are yet justly regarded by us as the work of God who set the conditions and gave the energy by which a long development should be accomplished; if the mountain is his handiwork, which ice and wind and rain have been fashioning for countless milleniums, it need not be thought that the moral law is less divine because it is not the work of a day.

We therefore find it true, though perhaps in a sense which the writer in Exodus did not intend to convey, that God spake these words. He spoke them earlier than he is here stated to have done; he spoke them from eternity, and gave to man a conscience to recognise their obligation. Man was left to learn them by experience. But he did learn them: all his efforts after settled life brought these laws to the surface as indispensable conditions of his welfare. In every country they appeared: when once they were discovered and declared, the conscience never failed to own them, and they became laws not of states only, but laws compelling with a force which states could not confer on them, the private thoughts and purposes of individual men. They thus possess an incomparable majesty such as no counsels of prudence, no mere maxims of experience, no social conventions can have; being declared by God, the author of human nature, the founder of all human commonwealths, not only to the Jews but to all men, not only at Mount Sinai but from the beginning of human life in the world.

III.

THE FIRST COMMANDMENT.

Thou shalt have no other Gods before me.

The commandments are not addressed to individuals, but to a nation. The "thou" to whom they speak is the people of Israel, and they are prefaced by a sentence, in which Jehovah states how it is his right to give laws to Israel. By bringing them out of the land of Egypt, out of the house of bondage, he has established a claim on them which they can never disown. And he now lays down the conditions on which he will continue to be their God, and to extend to them his favour and protection. The ten commandments, so we are to understand, are the conditions of that great alliance,—they constitute the terms of the covenant between Jehovah and Israel. The people agreed so to regard them; and in after times they felt that as long as they kept these laws they might count upon God as their defender, and might justly expect to be free and prosperous. When they broke these laws they lost the secret of prosperity, and did not fail to learn that their helper had departed from their side.

What is recognised so clearly, and expressed in such a dramatic form in the case of Israel, is true of every nation. There are certain fundamental conditions, it is well known, which every nation must observe if it is to prosper, which every nation that maintains itself in the world must at one time or another, expressly or silently, have accepted. And the ten commandments are, with certain slight exceptions, a part of those universal conditions of national well-being. They are addressed not only to Israel but to all nations: no nation can neglect them with safety, they form the foundation of all states.

The first of these conditions of national well-being, is that a nation must be true to its religion. If Moses gave this commandment, it required that Israel should not mix up different religions together, but remain constant to its own faith. In the age of the prophets it assumed a deeper meaning and came to demand not a practice only but a belief. The Israelites were now taken bound to believe that there is only one God, and to deny the existence of any other gods beside Jehovah.

A little historical reflection will enable us to understand how the meaning of the first commandment must vary according to the period of Jewish history, at which we suppose it to have been given. The great doctrine of monotheism, the view that Jehovah was the only God, and that the gods of the heathens had no real existence, was only arrived at by the prophets. Before the days of Amos and Hosea, the Jews were not monotheists, but believed in the existence of a number of deities, and it is unreasonable to suppose a law to have been imposed on them, forbidding belief in other gods, before that law had become natural and necessary to them. If, therefore, the commandment is the work of Moses or of an early age of Jewish history, it does not deny the existence of other gods, but it forbids the Israelites to worship them. This may be considered to be the original meaning of its words. It requires the nation to be true to the national religion, and not mix up foreign worships with it. It is an appeal to the national consciousness, to the sentiment of patriotism, and forbids other worships, because for Israel they are unpatriotic and unhistorical. If on the contrary the commandment is taken as the utterance of the prophetic age, which gave the Decalogue its present form, then it denies the existence of other gods, and forbids other worships because they are false, and are addressed to beings who are no gods, and have no real existence.

The commandment therefore requires faithfulness—

1. To the national religion.
2. To the true religion.

The second of these injunctions is far more important than the first: indeed it might almost be said that the first was abrogated when the second was arrived at. We need not dwell long on the older meaning of the commandment, but we cannot entirely pass it by.

1.

For a long time the Jews saw no harm in worshipping a number of deities side by side. When they entered Canaan they found it natural to worship the old gods of the land at the sacred spots with which it was studded, adding their own worship of Jehovah to that of the deities of the Canaanites which they found prevailing there. This went on for centuries; and in later times foreign deities were also introduced by several of the kings. Solomon sets up at Jerusalem an extensive collection of foreign cults; Ahab allows his wife, if the historian is to be believed, to convert to her religion, which she has imported, nearly the whole of his subjects. From the account of the reign of Manasseh at a much later period, and even from the prophecies of Ezekiel and Jeremiah, we see how natural it was to the Jews to engage in a number of different religions simultaneously. The tastes, which in our own day lead people to run after any violent and sensational style of worship, led the Israelites to run after Baal and Ashtoreth. The mystic excitement which accompanied the worship of these beings exercised an attraction which the quieter worship of Jehovah, born of the stillness and grandeur of the desert, could not compete with. It was long before the Jews overcame this tendency. Down to the exile the first commandment is that with which they are most frequently reproached with breaking.

But their own religion was to them what no other could be—the first, the best, their own. In it only did they remember their own history, in it only were they strong; they could only conquer when in living and active alliance with their own God. Away from him they forgot the reason of their separate existence as a nation: they became like the surrounding peoples, and were in danger of being absorbed, as the ten tribes actually were, in populations far inferior to themselves. When they revived as a nation it was because their religion revived. Every great leader they had was an enthusiast for the national religion, and led them to victory by reminding them of their ancestral covenant with Jehovah, and of their destiny to conquer and succeed in alliance with him. When they came back to Jehovah, after a period of distress or of subjection to a foreigner, they were near the end of their troubles. Their strength revived; they felt themselves again to be a nation, they recovered confidence in their future. In league with Jehovah they knew that they could never be conquered.

The experience of Israel in this is typical of all nations. Religion is the life-blood of every state, the mainspring of all institutions and all policy. And fickleness in religion is the most dangerous symptom a nation can exhibit. We also must, as we value our national existence, remain true to the God of our fathers, not necessarily to all their beliefs about him, but to the view by which they were inspired of their calling and their duty. Our beliefs we must change in the light of the new knowledge which is streaming upon us from all sides; but religion is more than a set of beliefs, and when we prove untrue to the religious spirit of our fathers, to the moral genius of our race, then the day of our fall will be at hand. While we remain faithful to the convictions of our fathers, we may feel sure that the God of our fathers will prosper our commonwealth. We need not hesitate to adopt some of the phraseology of Israel as to the alliance which exists between a nation and its god, nor scruple to believe and to act on the conviction that our national life also is in some respect divine, and that we are not only permitted but bound to do everything we can to preserve unimpaired our Empire and our national efficiency. Our race also is a chosen people, our battles also the battles of the Lord, our laws and order also his statutes: while we remain in living contact with him and allow no other power to shape our aims and conduct, we cannot fail to prosper.

2.

In the age of the prophets the commandment began to have another meaning. Reading the works of these great men we see the magnificent truths of theism rising in the minds of Israel, and the religion of a tribe becoming a religion for the world. Jehovah, formerly a national God who could be compared with the gods of other tribes, became to the prophets a being who was above all gods, and could have no rival. As Jehovah, the righteous and true God rose in the thoughts of

Israel to be first the greatest of all gods, and then the only God, the creator and governor of all the hosts of heaven and all the nations of the earth, the other beings who had been called gods lost first their rank, as they fell far below him, and then their very existence, as the conviction grew that there was no room in the world for more gods than one. All power was in Jehovah's hands, and the history of all nations was shaped and controlled by him, with a view to the fulfilment of his great purposes. The religion of Israel now assumed an air of exclusiveness which it had not hitherto worn. When the clear truth of a subject rises into view, and its necessity and majesty are recognised, there is one kind of charity which ceases to be possible. Those who are sure that they possess the truth of any matter, can no longer allow that other opinions on that matter are equally legitimate; and where the true religion has appeared, other forms of religion must of necessity, till philosophy appears, be regarded as false and vain. If Jehovah was the only god possessing any real existence, then Israel was obliged to condemn all worships but his own as baseless and untrue. It was easy to tolerate other religions before, when it was believed that the world was parcelled out among a number of deities, each claiming with equal right to be worshipped by his own people on his own ground; but if there was no God but one, that kind of toleration could be practised no longer. To depart from Jehovah became not only a sin but a folly; not only an unpatriotic but a stupid and irrational act. All other gods were idols and vanities; Jehovah, the righteous law-giver and just judge, was the only God, his service the only true religion. And the first commandment thus became a wall of separation between Israel and the surrounding peoples.

But the new views of God, while making it impossible for the Jews to tolerate other religions, gave them a deeper interest than they ever felt before in other peoples. They soon came to see that the worship of a God who was perfectly good and holy, could not be meant only for one nation, but that all nations must be summoned to take part in it. The writings of the prophets, and many of the Psalms, reflect the bright glow of the dawn of a universal religion. Many a great passage remains to show how wonderful the truth was when it first appeared, and how it made new the whole face of nature, and the whole of the thoughts and the experience of man. It was a greater discovery than that of a new continent upon the world's face, or of a force of nature hitherto unknown, when, after centuries of irritating and resultless conflicts of rival local deities, men found themselves in the presence of a being who was almighty and eternal, the Creator of all the ends of the earth. From that time they felt that religion need contain no element of darkness or unreason, that it was a matter on which it was to be expected that all nations would agree. Man was delivered from the doubt and misery of worshipping any being who was not certainly supreme, and had found a being worthy of entire devotion, trusting in whom even the frail children of the dust were superior to misfortune, and felt themselves to be engaged in a cause which could not fail.

The first commandment expressed to that age in the form of a dogma, this result of the prophetic thinking. In addition to the appeal to national and patriotic sentiment which it had always contained, the commandment now conveyed an appeal to truth and reason themselves, which it had contained before in a much less degree. It now spoke not of a practice merely but of a belief. The other gods of whom it spoke had no existence, no other God was present to the universe but that one righteous and merciful being in whom Israel had trusted: he was the Creator and Ruler of all things, and beside him there was no god, no saviour.

The commandment which bids us believe in one God who is supreme and infinite, is no mere arbitrary dogma, addressed in ancient times to a single people. It was present from the first in the heart and conscience of man, though it was long before he made out its meaning. It expresses a law of human thought which is binding on all men, and all who partake of man's reasonable nature may properly be summoned to join in worshipping the Almighty and most righteous God. In two ways chiefly the belief in such a Being is brought near to the children of men. They know him from his works, as the Almighty, the Creator, because the universe attests in all its parts the presence of one originating and indwelling mind, of one who faints not, neither is weary. They know him also from their own consciences, which tell them as outward nature cannot, of a righteous and holy lawgiver and judge, from whose presence they can never flee while they have any existence. And mind and conscience equally require that the Creator and the Lawgiver should be regarded as one and the same: that the God of nature should be held to be holy and just, and the God of conscience almighty and allwise. Heart and mind alike require us to believe in one great being, the centre and source of all perfections, and to consider that there is no power outside him, and none able, save in appearance, to resist him. In this belief Christianity has made no change: Christ only presents it to us in a more winning form. Without such a belief in the unity and the purpose of all things, and in the law addressed to us by a higher than merely human authority, man's mind cannot be satisfied nor his heart comforted, nor can his duty be made clear to him. This faith alone is able, as the greatest of the prophets said of it, to give power to the faint, to increase strength to them that have no might. The commandment is spoken to us also, is spoken to all men, and requires them in the name of outward nature, and of their own nature as human beings, in the name of the unity of thought, and of that just pride which forbids them to worship any being who is not supreme and infinite, in the name of human happiness and of social order and peace, not to depart from this faith which we have received. We are not forbidden to improve that faith, to work it out into more reasonable forms, to harmonize it with every part of our growing knowledge; in the second commandment indeed we are forbidden to enclose it in any fixed symbol so as to put a limit to its growth; but we are forbidden to desert it for any other faith, or to give up the first place in our minds to any other power than the righteous and almighty God.

Nor is the commandment superfluous in the days in which we live. There are other beings set up even now besides the God of our fathers, and we are invited to turn away from him to them. They are not called gods; men are so anxious to get rid of everything that bears that name. Nor are they worshipped; some of them at least are not suitable for that purpose, and men are anxious to get rid of worship. But they are put in the highest place and they practically shape the lives of those who put them there. There are those who put matter instead of God, and hold that matter is able to do everything and does everything that is done in this universe. To them there is no spirit prescribing to the world a spiritual end and guiding it to an unseen spiritual goal, and the human spirit need seek no converse with any power higher than itself. To those who think in this way duty cannot be divine; there is no authority above man to give him any laws, and what he calls duty is his own invention. It is inevitable that those who regard duty in such a way should care less about it. If men and nations are not called by a higher power to fulfil certain objects in the world, then there is no immutable reason why they should deny themselves anything they can attain, or should not simply do their best for themselves. To the worship of matter, therefore, the worship of expediency is near akin, a worship which in a thousand ways tempts the servants of the Most High to forsake him. The Chaldeans of old are reproached by one of the Hebrew prophets with sacrificing to their net and burning incense to their drag, because by them their portion was increased and their meat made plenteous; and where no divine law is recognised, it is not wonderful if men become slaves to the pleasures and successes of this world, and failing to realise the presence of God, bow down to the golden calf. Those whom such low worships cannot satisfy, become the prey, in the absence of spiritual objects and beliefs, of a dark spirit which tells them that there is nothing worth doing in this world, nothing to be hoped for, no true happiness, no substantial gain to be aspired after. The enthusiasms and hopes of a spiritual religion, they regard as idle, self-sacrifice and selfishness as alike vain and objectless. This religion of dreariness, of the absence of all true interests, also claims in our day thousands of votaries.

Where such beliefs creep in, social disorder and disorganisation are not far behind. The respect which is denied to the laws of God will not be paid to the ordinances of man. Recognising no authority above the world, the members of the state will know no object but their own interests, no law but their own will. In departing from religion they have lost the bond which holds them together as a nation; and they will cease to make sacrifices for the public good, because they can no longer realise the spiritual nature of human life, or the divine vocation of their race.

From all such services of foreign and strange vanities may God himself of his mercy set us free. May grace and courage be given to us to believe in the righteous God in whom our fathers trusted, to hearken to the call he addresses to us, and to reverence his laws. To be assured of a divine government of the world, and in a wise purpose, far-off perhaps, but sure, to which all things are tending, is, so far as belief goes, the secret of vigour and of happiness; to support that government, to help, though it be ever so little, the accomplishment of that purpose, is the part to which all men are called; and those who attempt to second the

Deity in the work he is doing for mankind, know that their strength increases in his service, and that they do not labour in vain.

THE SECOND COMMANDMENT.

Thou shalt not make unto thee any graven image: thou shalt not bow down thyself to them nor serve them.

THIS commandment marks the sacrifice the Jewish nation made, in order to preserve its spiritual treasure. To maintain the belief in one invisible God, who was far above the world, the use of images in religion had to be forsworn, even of such images as were meant to represent him and to lead the thoughts to him. Moses caused his people to enter into covenant with a God who, it was felt more and more as time went on, was not to be reached by any of the senses, but only by the efforts of the mind; and the history of Israel during many centuries is mainly a record of the struggles made by men who were full of that national conception of the Deity, to keep their people also true to it, in spite of the fact that other modes of worship were easier. Especially did the great prophets enforce the prohibition of images with a strictness unknown to Moses, or to the centuries succeeding him: under their influence the brazen serpent was broken to pieces which Moses himself had made; and the calves or bulls which Elijah had tolerated became the symbols of a terrible defection from the true faith. Religion came to regard certain forms of art with suspicion, or with positive hostility. Art was left without the impulse of religion, under which her greatest triumphs, both in ancient and in modern times, have been achieved; and religion lost the enrichment and illustration which art is fitted to lend her. Art did little for the Jews, and their religion was stiff and austere.

If the object aimed at was attained, it was worth the sacrifice. If Israel was enabled ultimately to clear from all confusion the spiritual conception of God set forth at first by Moses, and to present that idea to the world as a fixed and imperishable possession, the race which did such a work has earned the eternal gratitude of mankind. The question, however, may now arise whether, where a spiritual view of God has taken complete hold of men's minds, the need for such a commandment as this, and for all the jealous watchfulness which accompanies it, has not passed away? Has such an injunction any fitness when addressed to the Christian people of an age in which religion is no longer afraid of art, but has learned to employ her as a handmaid? When we read the ten commandments in church, might we not, so far as any practical purpose is to be gained, omit this one?

If we regarded the letter of the commandment merely, we might find this to be the case. The acts which it forbids are not acts which the members of Protestant churches, in this country at least, are at all likely to do. The Roman Catholic Church by the sanction which it gives to image worship, practically sets aside the second commandment: but this has led Protestants to uphold it with even an exaggerated fervour. To make an image of anything in the creation, and fall down before it expecting something from it, is the last thing we should ever think of doing. Such an action is repugnant to all our habits of thought; we see too clearly the absurdity which it involves. Not in this way are we at all likely to be entangled in idolatry, so that it should be necessary for us to banish art from our religion, in order to keep our religion pure.

Yet it may be the case that the tendency which led Moses to make a brazen serpent, and Aaron a golden bullock, the tendency to render religion easy by making its object fixed and visible, is still at work, though with us it finds different modes of expressing itself from those of old times. That tangible portable deities are absurd and ludicrous we have by this time learned; but there are other ways of making religion exact, and as it becomes exact, unspiritual; and if we are prone to any of these, this commandment may still convey to us a useful warning. That we may see if this is so, let us first of all inquire into the reasons of the prohibition of the simple idolatry of the early world. Why were the Jews forbidden to make images and worship them? When we have answered that question we shall be able to see if the second commandment contains a truth, which is not merely local and temporary, but applicable to all forms of religion at all times.

The reasons why the Jews were forbidden to

make any image of God are to be found very clearly and strongly stated in the second part of the book of Isaiah and in a number of the Psalms. The idols referred to in Isaiah are those of Babylon; but the ideas he expresses were held by earlier believers in Jehovah with regard to the idols of their day, and are the true explanation of the second commandment. The principal reason of the prohibition was that it was impossible to make any image which should be in any degree like God. An image is like some particular thing, but God is not like any particular thing. An image has the shape of a man, or of a bull, or of a fish; but all these are God's handiwork, and it is childish to think that he who made them all resembles any one of them rather than the rest. If, as the prophets came to believe, God is the Creator of all things, and gave them all alike their form and breath, then he cannot be figured in the shape of any of them without the grossest untruthfulness and irreverence. Again, to put God into an image is to make him small, smaller than the maker of the image. But if he made all things and men too, then he is so great that nothing man can make can in the least resemble him. To make an image of him is to misrepresent him. It is to make him small instead of great, finite instead of infinite, of a particular shape instead of everywhere and over all. It is to make him like other gods, who are represented by images of one thing or another, instead of being as he is, quite unlike these other Gods, of quite a different nature from theirs. And so however good the man's intentions were in making an image for himself, he has committed the greatest possible mistake. He acted, no doubt, from a pious and religious motive. He found it difficult to realise God's presence by the unaided efforts of his mind, he could not think of God satisfactorily without some outward assistance. He wanted to have God near him, to have God in his house, so that he might enjoy the constant sense of higher protection, and pay his vows to his protector daily. But in seeking thus to bring God near, the maker of the idol has run great risk of losing the true God altogether. He has in reality renounced the Infinite God in favour of a substitute, and exchanged the religion of the spirit for a bodily exercise. He has stereotyped his religion, and it must therefore inevitably degenerate. The image was perhaps intended to be no more than a symbol, and the worshipper may assure himself from time to time that it is no more than a sign of an unseen reality; but the weakness which required such an aid at first will learn increasingly to lean on it, and will grow content with the symbol and forget the greater being symbolised. Not seeking God in his own mind the image-worshipper fails to learn anything further about him. His religion will stand still, it will resist all growth and change, it will become more and more unreflective and mechanical, and will tend to weaken and embarrass, instead of elevating and encouraging him.

These are the reasons which the Bible gives for the prohibition of images. They prevent the growth of religion. They remove it from the mind, in which it ought to have its seat, and make it a transaction which demands no thought. They check the progress of the knowledge of God, and degrade the worshipper from a thinking being to a being who is not called to think. And this will be found to be the effect of the use of images wherever it prevails. Those who have lived in Catholic countries and have witnessed the simple and intense devotion paid to images, which are far from possessing any artistic merit, on the roadsides and in the churches, will not be forward to condemn such worship. More fervent piety, more pathetic appeals to higher beings for sorely needed blessings, you will nowhere see than in the churches of Roman Catholic Belgium or Germany. But the religion of these countries is one which makes no progress and exercises little influence on men of activity and intellect. Religion once attached to outward objects stands still; it is packed in a system which the priests work according to rule, and which the people observe best when their mind is not brought actively to bear on it. The more enlightened spirits of the nation are estranged from religion in such circumstances: it breeds scepticism, there can be no advance, at least within the church, to nobler views of God and of man's destiny, till the images are put out of the way. Religion carried on by means of images becomes an obstruction to human progress, a positive hindrance to the spirit in its search after God.

Where, however, the danger does not exist that the use of outward symbols in connection with religion will hinder the growth of the spirit, the reason for this commandment disappears. The evil is not in the making but in the worshipping; if there is no danger of the latter, the former is innocent. Among Protestants, who have learned for centuries to keep religion living in their minds by allowing their judgment to play upon it, and who regard the preaching of the Word as the central and effectual part of the worship of God, it is a question of taste rather than of principle, in what way and to what extent, art shall be brought in to serve religion. The superstition which would prevent us from employing the resources of art in the decoration of our churches, we need scarcely notice. The great fact which public worship celebrates and symbolises, the meeting of God with men, his dwelling among them, he their God, and they his people, is a fact so touching and so wonderful that we can never do too much in seeking to make the expression of it worthy. Some may prefer simplicity, some ornament; it is a question to be settled according to the tastes of those concerned. As long as it is kept in mind that the central fact of worship is a movement of thought, and not a mechanical operation, it will appear to many that no human faculty can justly be shut out from contributing to it, which can bring to it any suitable gift. And it might therefore be thought that this commandment has discharged its office for us, that this portion of the law is dead for us, long ago.

But the commandment is not dead for us. It contains a different message from that which it carried to the Israelites, but it still utters the same principle, and warns us against the idols of a more intellectual age. There are other images than those which are made of wood and stone, and decked with tinsel,— images not seen with the bodily eye, but set up for worship in the mind, clung to with the most extreme tenacity, and too often standing between the soul and God, and hindering the growth of true religion. Perhaps it is inevitable that we should try to frame some picture in our minds of the Being to whom we address our prayers. Without having some picture of this sort many would be apt to feel that they had no God at all. If seeing is believing, it appears to many that some mental vision of God, at least, is necessary, if they are to have any assurance about him. All the language in which we speak about him is pictorial and fitted to suggest mental images. At times of religious excitement, such as occur in every life, vivid images suggested by the current theology, are produced before the mind's eye, and to these we naturally cling in after times, as they are connected with our most memorable experiences.

But when any particular picture of God becomes fixed and stereotyped in the belief of a people, it becomes a danger to religion. When a current view of God's character and dealings is set up as a view which is delivered to us by the highest authority, and which is never to be changed, there we see the manufacture of an image, possessing all the defective and mischievous qualities of those composed of grosser substance. When it is given out that those who would come to God must come to him through that representation, and that those who reject that representation are without God, then we see the production on the one hand of the mechanical and superstitious worship, on the other of the scepticism and alienation of active minds, which are inseparable from the setting up of images. An idol has been set up which must be broken before the worship of God in spirit and truth can prevail. Our forefathers conceived of God as dwelling in a certain district of the sky, as wielding the thunderbolt with his own hands, as interfering frequently with the course of nature to punish offenders, as dictating to the sacred writers the words now printed in the Bible. To us, whose views of the universe have been so marvellously extended by scientific discoveries, God must be much greater than he was to our forefathers, and his government must be much more steadfast and regular than they conceived it. The god in whom they believed is not great enough to fill the throne of the universe such as we now know it to be. This is an illustration, perhaps the greatest illustration, of the principle we are speaking of. To seek to retain that old way of thinking of God, or any view that has grown too small, or is found repugnant to a more developed moral sentiment; to insist that we must either believe in God in that antiquated fashion, or count ourselves to be without him, this is not a procedure that is either honouring to God or likely to promote faith in him. The idols of the mind are not less dangerous than their simpler predecessors of wood and stone, nor less surely fated to be broken and cast away.

We saw that the first commandment bids us be true to our religion, and not desert it for any other. The second commandment, rightly understood, bids us forbear from interfering with the growth of that religion by fixing it in cramped and narrow forms. If religion is to continue to be what it was in former periods of our history, a bond of national unity and an inspirer of national enthusiasm, it must now seek to be in sympathy with the growing knowledge and thought of the age, and to cultivate such wide and comprehensive views of God and his dealings, that no class of men engaged in serious studies shall feel themselves shut out from its communion. It must be recognised that the search for truth is one of the highest and most essential parts of the service of God, and that truthfulness, displayed in whatever field and combined with whatever set of views, proves men holy and religious. There are other methods besides that of naked idolatry by which we may make our service of God unworthy of him and of our own knowledge and faculties. The blind worship of the Bible impedes the growth of spiritual religion as truly as the worship of an idol does; so does superstitions or time-serving adherence to a creed, so does the undue exaltation of the office of the ministry.

The God who made heaven and earth, and whose first and chief demands are righteousness, and truth, and purity, is not strict or punctilious as to the forms under which we think of him or worship him. But he demands that he shall be supreme, and that we should never think of him in such a way, never make him so small, that he should fail to occupy the first place in our view of the universe, and the first place in our hearts. The way to make our intercourse with him real and living is not to make him small by enclosing him in the stiff and imperfect forms of man's devising, but to stretch out our own thoughts towards him, and make them great and wide. He is present, is he not most truly present? in the mind which has cast away all pictures of him: true faith in his real and abiding presence may arise out of the despair, at first so agonizing to the soul, which has befallen our attempts to set him forth to our mind's eye, or to retain those ideas of him which are connected with our earliest memories. We think of him aright when we have learned to think that there is nothing outside him or beyond him or refractory to his designs, when we have learned to regard all human learning and discovery as proceeding from him, and the minds of all men, however variously and opposedly they may appear to work, as reflections of his infinite mind.

THE THIRD COMMANDMENT.

Thou shalt not take the name of the Lord thy God in vain.

SURELY it can matter little to the Divine Being how men treat his name. Nothing they can say about him, no slight they can cast on his name, can really affect him; no such occurrence, we should think, can either vex his mind or disturb his plans. The almighty and unchangeable can surely afford to disregard what is said of him by the weak and changeable, and to let their words, which can accomplish nothing, simply pass by.

But it matters a great deal to men that the divine name should be treated with reverence among them. Even if God's government is so firmly established that he has no need to keep a watch on the expressions used by his subjects, still it must always be a matter of the first importance that the respect and awe which surround God's name and all connected with the Deity, should be maintained. This men owe to each other; and even if we did not think that God gave us any such commandment as this, we should feel that the deepest interests of society imposed it upon us. To the pious heart there is no need of such a law; but it is clearly one of those which lay down the essential conditions of society, and it is given from heaven as clearly as any other for the benefit of men.

We may remark here that the offence which the third commandment suggests most readily to our minds, that of profane and ribald swearing, and the coarse use of words connected with religion in common conversation, was not that at which it was originally aimed. To that kind of disrespect for religion the Jews, with all their faults, were never addicted; they were given, as we shall see, rather to superstitious and exaggerated reverence for sacred things than to irreverence. They believed moreover, with the early world generally, that cursing was effectual, and this would necessarily cause it to be reserved for weighty occasions.

Where this belief prevailed, a habit of profanity could scarcely make its appearance. The habit which still prevails in this country is rather to be called thoughtless and indecent, than positively mischievous; those who indulge in it could never do so if they expected their words to have any effect. But if we consider what the offences were which the commandment was originally intended to condemn, we shall see that it applies with all its force to every form of disrespect for religion, that this hateful habit of profane swearing also falls under its sentence.

The name of Jehovah was to the early Hebrews the name by which they swore, or plighted their word to each other. When two people made a bargain they called upon Jehovah to witness it. Jehovah, they said, be between me and thee. Then they felt that their agreement was ratified. The name of God conferred on it a sacred character. He would watch over it, and his wrath would descend on the person who broke it. Thus the name of Jehovah was the seal of the covenant these persons made. It was because each of them believed that the fear of Jehovah was present in the mind of the other as it was present in his own, that they were able to make a bargain with each other in the belief that it would be carried out. But how, if a man should come to negotiate with another, and make a bargain with him, and pretend to seal it with the name of Jehovah, while all the time he had no intention of keeping it, but was simply seeking to lead the other party into a trap? This was to take Jehovah's name in vain. We may remark that some good authorities regard this as the original application of the third commandment. This was to use God's great and holy name for unworthy ends, to turn the efficacy which was in it, the confidence placed in it by the community, into an instrument of fraud. No wonder that this is declared to be a commandment the breach of which Jehovah could not tolerate. It was not to be endured that, when called on to witness a bargain, He should be made to assist in an act of deception. And so it is expressly added to this commandment, that Jehovah will not hold him guiltless who taketh his name in vain. He may escape punishment from men, the *Shorter Catechism* says, but God will not suffer him to escape his righteous judgment.

Thus in requiring respect for religion the third commandment is defending the sacredness of the bargains and engagements men make with each other; and the threat added to it is not directed against irreverence merely, but against faithlessness and perjury. It protects society by a solemn religious sanction against a great danger. If the name of Jehovah was not kept sacred, so the Hebrews felt, if men were to be at liberty to use it to overreach those they were dealing with, then confidence would be at an end. Men would cease to make bargains with each other, which the other party, though he used the name of Jehovah, might have no intention of keeping: and if bargains ceased to be made, society would travel back to the primitive stage at which every man has to do everything he wants done, for himself. Thus the fear of God's name was one of the deepest foundations of society; if the fear of God's name was not kept up, society was in danger of falling to pieces.

Now there can be no doubt that this is still the

case. It is still the existence of religion among men that enables them to place confidence in one another, and to make bargains with each other in the faith that these engagements will be carried out. It is because I believe that my fellow-man has the fear of God before his eyes, that he has a conscience as well as I have, that he feels himself as I do, to be in the presence of an unseen power, which forbids him to speak falsely or act fraudulently, and which he knows will punish him if he does so speak or act, it is because I believe my fellow-man to have the same things in his mind in these respects as I myself have, that I trust him and make bargains with him. Any man whom I believed to be destitute of religion in this sense, any man whom I suspected of having no reverence for the moral law, no fear of God, I should not deal with in a matter demanding any confidence. The presence of religion in the minds of others is my security in dealing with them. Where religion is deep and living, people will be disposed to trust each other. Where there is little religion, or, what amounts to the same thing, where a religion prevails which is taken up with formalities of worship, or with selfish ecstacies, or with political propagandism, rather than the weightier matters of justice and truth and self-control; there little confidence will be possible among men, and the social fabric will be less secure.

Thus to any one who is interested even in the industrial and commercial prosperity of the country, it cannot be a matter of indifference that religion should be a living and active force in men's hearts. It is vital to the welfare of any country that in the great matters of practical morality the minds of its citizens should be at one, that they should believe with one consent in the supreme obligations which rest upon them to be just and true. In the name of our fellow-creatures whom religion teaches so to live that they may dwell together in mutual trust and helpfulness, as well as in the name of God on whom we depend for inward comfort and strength, we are forbidden to say anything or do anything to weaken the power of religion. Religion is what binds us to our fellowmen: it is what we have in common with them all, what dwells in the minds of all of us alike. However much we differ from them in other respects, in rank, in character, in the opinions we hold and the objects we pursue, there speaks in their hearts as in ours a voice which tells us for what end we have come here, and what duties we are bound to fulfil while we are here. That is what makes us one, and enables us to live and act together. And any words or acts that tend to cast disrespect upon that common element in all our lives, and to loosen the hold which the eternal Righteousness exerts on us, is fatally injurious both to ourselves and to those among whom we live.

And therefore all the forms in which we worship God or in which others worship him ought to be sacred in our eyes. We ought not to speak lightly of any thing that pertains to religion, because religion is what declares to us and to our fellow-creatures the claims of duty. We ought to regard with respect even those beliefs and rites which for our own part we cannot adopt, and which we see to be mistaken. If they form the channels of religious influence to any fellow-creatures, we cannot scorn them; for though the vessels may be earthen, the treasure that is in them is divine.

The Jews afford the most striking example that could possibly be given of the fact that reverence may be misdirected. They interpreted this commandment in a superstitious way. Being forbidden to take the name of God in vain, they came to think, in an age long after Moses, that it was safer not to use the divine name at all. They ceased to utter it, and when in reading the Bible they came to the word Jehovah, the name of God, they pronounced another word instead of it. They regarded it as possessing a magic power which might dart forth upon them and hurt them if they handled it incautiously.

And in other particulars also they carried the tendency to regard divine things with awe to great excess. They fenced in religion with a multitude of regulations and prohibitions meant to keep men at a distance from the object of their worship, and to mark off the sacred as strongly as possible from the secular. To judge by the religion they practised in the time of Jesus, they regarded God as a dreadful and jealous potentate, who by a thousand rites and observances kept man from coming too near him, and whom it was very dangerous to approach without great caution. Jesus was accused of blasphemy because his intimate sense of God's presence and goodness led him to disregard the fences and restrictions with which religion was encumbered in his day, and to take up towards God the attitude of nearness and confidence which befits a son in his intercourse with a Father.

The Jewish spirit still lives, though perhaps its power is waning. Even in our own country we may witness the display of an exaggerated reverence under which the service of God is turned into mere terror and restraint, instead of being, as it should, the joy and encouragement of man's heart. Man has often shewn his weakness and shews it still, by making religion a yoke and a slavery to forbidding and inaccessible powers, of a different nature from his own, instead of a reasonable intercourse with a being who made man in his own image. The things of God are often held to form a supernatural domain in which reason and criticism must keep silence, and the ideas and habits of liberty be forgotten.

But this is a misapplication of reverence. God is not an Oriental despot to be served in so abject a fashion; his commandments are reasonable, his service is perfect freedom. He is a Father who desires to have his children at his side, and delights in the growth of their intelligence, which enables them to find out his ways and to understand his counsel. When speaking of the Second Commandment, which forbids us to make any image of God, we saw the reason of that prohibition to be that a fixed form, whether made by the hands or by the ingenious minds of men, arrests the growth of religion and makes it stiff and mechanical. The same consideration shows that the fear of God of which this commandment speaks must not be a fear which paralyses the working of our minds or keeps us at a great distance from him. The duty of treating religion with reverence cannot relieve us of the obligation to enquire into the truth of religious doctrines, and to seek to make our religious views as far as possible such as may claim the assent of all men.

There is no irreverence in the attempt to modify and develop religious beliefs, so as to fit them to become more universal. The truest reverence indeed would dictate the removal from religion of any elements in her which we see to be temporary in their nature, and ceasing to satisfy the intelligence of men, so that she may shine forth again in her native youth and beauty

"Free from semblance of decline."

God dwells not in temples made with hands or in doctrines of men's devising, and it has often been seen that those had most real reverence for divine things who spoke against the established notions about them. So did the ancient prophets, so also did Jesus, and so also the great Reformer, Luther.

Yet at a time of difficulty in religion like the present it becomes all good and earnest men to treat sacred subjects carefully and tenderly, so that if there must needs be change, there may yet if possible be no substantial loss, of that which more than anything else cements society together. Especially is there great need to resist that shallow and conceited spirit which wonders at nothing and reverences nothing, and pushes itself forward into the most sacred places with laughter and sneers. To treat with levity what our fellow-creatures worship is a sin which it is hard to atone for. To speak lightly of beliefs which were cherished by our parents and which are still the refuge of thousands of devout hearts, is at once a hard-hearted and a stupid act, insulting to others, and banishing the person guilty of it to a cold solitude. This is the offence against all that is holy and profound in human life which cannot be forgiven, from which when once it has been committed it is most difficult to recover. Reverence is the breath of life to the soul; without it there is no life, no progress, no communion with God, no helpful fellowship with men. When reverence dies the soul is dead: no growth awaits her, none but material objects will be her care, no heavenly influence will come to make her young again, no living spring of hope burst forth in her. The laughter of the fool to whom nothing is sacred, nothing dear, is a dearly purchased pleasure.

May a sweeter and more natural frame of mind be ours. Man is made to look up to God and to live with the fear of God upon him. The love we feel to God casts out the fear which is slavish and superstitious, and allows us still to hold up our head and to respect ourselves, though we are in his presence; but it does not cast out that better fear, the sweet submission, the willing reverence which the lower must always feel towards the higher, the child to the father. The father who is best loved is most reverenced, because he bears the fullest sway over his child's heart, and the child cannot think of slighting or opposing him. Life is worth having if it is filled with reverence; a life that looks up to nothing is not worth living. Let us have the Lord always before us, let us see him in all things, let a deep and noble reverence for the eternal holiness and truth and mercy go with us everywhere. Then our lives will be full of interest, and hope will never forsake us.

THE FOURTH COMMANDMENT.

Remember the Sabbath day to keep it holy.

It has always been felt that this commandment stands on a somewhat different footing from the others, and that its presence in the Decalogue requires to be explained. The other nine commandments impose nothing that men have not learned in various other ways to be binding upon them. The duties they enjoin are such as reason itself imposes, and are recognised and enforced, generally speaking, in all lands. There is nothing capricious, nothing that time or place may change, in the laws which command us to be faithful to the true religion, to worship God in a spiritual manner, and to hold his name in reverence; nor in those which enforce the duties of morality towards our fellow creatures; these laws are suited for all men everywhere, and justify themselves to every thinking mind. The fourth commandment stands on a different footing. It speaks of an institution which was peculiar to Israel among the prominent nations of antiquity, and one of the principal effects of which was to make the Israelite peculiar in whatever country he might dwell. It is true that other nations besides the Jews had a week of seven days, and the institution of the seventh day's festival. But it is in the Jewish religion alone that we find this institution lifted into such prominence and put forward as one of the principal parts of man's duty to God. Is a week of seven days intrinsically better or more moral than one of eight days or of ten, such as some ancient nations observed, or does conscience dictate that on the weekly festival we should abstain from work and from all worldly occupations? We cannot assert that the Jewish practice in this respect is one naturally incumbent on all men. More convenient, more healthy, more elevating it may have been than other practices; but few would be found to assert that it is one which, apart from the Bible, must necessarily be recognised as universally right and binding.

We must therefore acknowledge that the fourth commandment possesses a lower degree of authority than the other nine. It is not a precept of natural religion, nor a law which has come to be respected in all countries. And with this it agrees that our Lord himself speaks of it in language which he would never have applied to any of the others. His words express in the most pointed way the difference which exists between it and them. Man was not made for the Sabbath, he says. Man was created for spiritual religion, for reverence to the Most High, for control of his passions, for purity, for honesty, for truthfulness: the laws which require these of him were eternal laws before he came to know them; he did not invent them, he cannot change them, he has no choice but to obey them. But he was not created for the Sabbath. In this institution there is nothing necessary or eternal. The ends it serves might have been served in other ways. Man is older and more venerable than it is, and entitled to more consideration. The Sabbath was made for man.

When the institution of the seventh days' rest is based as it is by our Lord on the ground of its usefulness, the task of defending it is easy. A commandment or institution which is not intrinsically reasonable is a great weakness to religion. Superstition fastens by preference on such an arbitrary ordinance, and insists chiefly upon the sacrifice which is humiliating and purposeless, to the neglect of those which are reasonable and beneficent. When religion is thus made to consist largely of observances which have no inherent reasonableness to recommend them, it is exposed to the easy taunts of the scoffer, who imputes to religion itself all the exaggerations of its votaries.

Not to insist upon the fact that the Christian Sunday is not the Sabbath of the Jews at all, and grew up in Christianity independently of the Sabbath and from quite different motives, the seventh day's rest which we possess as well as the Jews, ought to be based on the right grounds. It would be well to give up the attempt to place an observance which our Lord spoke of as a matter of utility only, and which the apostle Paul declared to be an element of religion which Christians had outgrown, on the same level with the primary obligations of righteousness, and to content ourselves with shewing how useful it has been and still is, to mankind. If the weekly rest be a gift which, as Christ declares, God has given to man during the course of his history to use for his best advantage, then men ought not to be driven into compliance with the traditional rules which have gathered round it, but should be left free to use the legacy in the way they find to be most profitable for them. Men will not readily part with so precious a birthright; if they find that it is theirs to dispose of they will not fail, broadly speaking, to turn it to the best advantage. Of this as of all other possessions it may be said that to make the best use of it we must feel our right to it secure. To speak of Sunday as a divine gift to man and then go on to say that he is bound to use it in a certain way, is to create suspicion of a gift which is so hampered. If we give up all attempt to enforce a certain way of spending the day, there is no doubt that the motives which have caused such an institution to spring up and to flourish over so large a portion of the globe, will continue to operate, so that the day will be jealously guarded, and turned, on the whole, to the best use.

But let us ask what is the essence of the institution which the fourth commandment confirmed for the Jews, and which we possess in the Christian Sunday.

1. It is a respite from toil.

It is in this light that the prophets regard the observance of the Sabbath, as soon as they come to take an interest in the subject. It is not too much to say that the earlier prophets take little interest in the Sabbath; they even find fault with their countrymen for excessive attention to the day. Hosea is so far from regarding the Sabbath as an eternal and necessary part of religion that he can speak of God's bringing about its discontinuance, along with that of the new moon festivals, which he places in the same category with it (ii. 11.), and Isaiah speaks (i. 13.) of the punctilious observance of the day as a piece of superstition, which could do nothing to recommend the people to Jehovah. The prophets could scarcely have spoken of the Sabbath in this way had they regarded it as an eternal and necessary part of religion. The reason of their contemptuous expressions is that in the time of these writers the

Sabbath was, like the new moon and other feasts, a day of sacrifice, not, as it afterwards became, a day of prayer. It thus ministered to the tendency of the Jews to make religion consist in outward acts of worship, which the cruel and impure could do as well as the gentle and the pure, rather than in righteousness and mercy.

The later prophets, however, spoke of the Sabbath in a very different strain. They saw in this ancient habit of their people of separating the seventh day of the week from the other six, a useful instrument of pure religion, and they did their best to infuse into it a higher meaning and a more humane spirit than it had possessed before. In ancient times the Sabbath had been a day of sacrifice, and of the happy social intercourse accompanying sacrifice. In the darker days before the exile, it had been a day of sombre and elaborate rites, a day for men to afflict their souls. Jeremiah (chap. xvii.), and the second Isaiah (chap. lvi., lviii.), declared that it ought to be a day of rest, a day on which a man's business should stand still, and his servants enjoy a holiday. The story of the creation in six days, which entered

Jewish literature about the Babylonian period, readily afforded a theological foundation for this view. In the fourth commandment as we now have it, the humane spirit of the prophets speaks through that story. The only law in the Decalogue which might be thought to be of a ceremonial nature, to deal with the externals of religion, is not inspired by a ceremonial motive. It ordains rest on the seventh day as a matter of philanthropy rather than of ritual. It does not impose a yoke, it is an edict of emancipation from a yoke. It is not directed against such an offence as making an excursion on the Sabbath: it is addressed to employers of labour, to heads of families, and commands them not to make their servants or even their animals, work on that holiday.

The liberal and benevolent character of the prophetic religion is very conspicuous here. To all toilers one day in seven is to be a holiday, every man and woman, and every beast of burden, living on the soil where the religion prevails, is to be entitled to this relaxation. Some parts of the Old Testament speak strongly of the constant and hopeless drudgery which has been the fate of so many of those who are made in God's image, and which has stirred so deeply the anger of poets and of orators. In the third chapter of Genesis man is told after his brief enjoyment of Eden, that it is his fate henceforward to eat his bread in the sweat of his brow, and to spend his life in a never-ending struggle with an ungrateful task, till death discharge him. But the fourth commandment proclaims his periodical emancipation from a life of drudgery. One day in seven he is to cease from his toil, to lift up his head from his task, and turn his mind to other thoughts. His holiday is not to depend on the state of his work nor on the indulgence of a master; the sun is to bring it round regularly every seventh day throughout the year. Six days he is to labour, but when the seventh day comes he is to be a free man. And masters are specially enjoined not to encroach upon the leisure their servants thus enjoy. The seventh is the working man's own day, and he is to be left free to use it as his own. In the commentary on the commandment in the book of

Deuteronomy, the Hebrew master is bidden to remember that Israel was once a bondsman in the land of Egypt, and should thus know how servants feel, and how precious the time is to them when they can lay down their tools. The Sabbath is a sacred possession which the servant has, and the master must not think of turning it to his own selfish advantage.

It would certainly be an exaggeration to say that if the fourth commandment had not been given we should have had no holidays. Nations which observed no weekly rest have yet had a number of regular holidays distributed throughout the year. Man's need for relaxation must be met in one way or another. But it is hard to imagine any system which would meet the claims both of labour and of relaxation so well as that which Christendom inherits from the Jews. It is a system which no nation that possessed it would ever consent to part with. No system could be better fitted to elevate the toilers of a country above a life of dull and cheerless drudgery. Sunday gives life another face for those who are chained all the week to their toil. It decks with a fringe of poetry the prose of necessary labour. It transports men into another sphere than that in which they earn their bread, and enables them to look upon the world from a position of dignity and freedom. It is not right, it is not to be tolerated in a Christian country, that any class should have such hard tasks or should be so ill paid, that the members of it cannot enjoy recreation with their families, nor realise their nature as intellectual beings. It is only when men are free from fatigue that their higher faculties unfold themselves. And it is such drudgery as stunts human nature and debars men and women from cultivation that the fourth commandment most directly condemns. It forbids unremitted toil; it protests against the degradation of human beings to mere instruments of industry, and requires that all men should enjoy a due portion of that repose of body without which the higher aptitudes of their nature, their social, reasonable, and spiritual faculties cannot get free. The factory legislation of the last half century is perhaps more directly in the spirit of the fourth commandment than the Sabbatarian efforts of that period. If sufficient rest is given, it matters little on what day of the week it is enjoyed. What the commandment says to us most emphatically is, that we are to allow no one who is dependent on us to be overwhelmed with labour or shut out from opportunities of relaxation.

2. The Sabbath was a rest in the Lord.

In the time of the exile, when the Jews were deprived of their temple and its sacrifices, and were forced to learn to worship God at a distance from his dwelling-place in Zion, the nature of their worship underwent a radical change. Prayer took the place of sacrifice; the splendid dramatic assemblages and acts of the temple were replaced by the prayer-meetings of the exile, the Psalms came into use, and those habits of spiritual worship were formed which, after the return to Palestine, gave rise to the system of the synagogue. The Sabbath partook of this great change: from a day of sacrifice it became a day of prayer, and from this time forward it was one of the principal outward distinctions of the Jewish people and religion. Wherever Jews were found throughout the world, they presented to their neighbours this striking peculiarity, that they rested from toil every seventh day, and engaged on that day in acts of social worship.

This we may call a new institution of the Sabbath, though it is not expressly described to us anywhere in the Bible; and in this new consecration it was a purely reasonable and spiritual observance. But it was not long before it ceased to be so. The Jews learned after the exile to draw hard and inflexible distinctions of an arbitrary kind between what was sacred and what was profane in every department of life, and to make holiness consist in separation from whatever religion had not selected as its own. The Sabbath now came to be regarded as essentially different from the other days of the week. It was a sacrifice which God required of man's time, and which man could not refuse. The first six days it was now supposed, were common, were man's, but the seventh day was God's, and man must not spend it as he liked; he must spend it in a particular manner which was prescribed, and offer it to God in the manner God ordained.

It was at this period accordingly, when the religion of the Jews was losing all its freshness and naturalness, when it was departing from the liberal and humane spirit of the prophets, and clothing itself in the stiff and artificial vestments of ritualism, that Sabbatarianism appeared among them. The manifold restrictions with which Sunday is still fenced about in this country, the distinctions between things which may be done and things which must not be done on that day, the conception that when twelve o'clock strikes on Saturday night we enter upon a region of time which is not ours to dispose of, and in which we must put on a different behaviour from that which is natural to us, this way of thinking is a legacy we inherit directly from the priests and scribes of later Judaism, along with many other sombre and oppressive notions.

The belief that one portion of time is more sacred than another is evidently one which Christians who are convinced that God, who has his dwelling in their heart, is with them everywhere and always, cannot entertain. If God is with us always, then no portion of our time is his more than the rest; it is all his alike. The clock cannot bring us near him, nor relieve us of his presence. The way to serve him with our time is not to give him special days, the rest remaining ours, but to give it all to him, and to live every day and always as in his eye. And those who think thus are free to denounce the tyranny of Sabbatarianism. So long as the rights of all workers to their weekly holiday are not infringed, every restriction on the spending of Sunday ought to be removed. If we recognise that all our time is equally sacred, we shall be no party to establishing or keeping up restrictions for other people, the validity of which we do not acknowledge for ourselves. And if we sympathise with the liberal and kindly spirit in which the fourth commandment was at first conceived, we shall not willingly curtail the value of the gift it makes to man by disputing his liberty to use it according to his best judgment. Should there ever be a danger of the abstraction from any class of their weekly rest, and should that class appear to be unable to defend its threatened privilege, we shall gladly do what we can to prevent such an act of spoliation. But we shall not readily be drawn into any movement for forcing any set of persons who are fit to judge of their own conduct and able to defend their rights, to spend Sunday in a particular way. May we lead in our crops on Sunday? it has recently been asked. By all means serve God on Sunday in that way, if you feel called on to do so; taking care, of course, not to encroach on the rights of any one. God would have you to judge of such matters for yourselves. And why should public collections be closed on that day, the day when working-men are most free to visit them, or why should you not walk in the fields on Sunday, and take your wives and children with you, and study natural history or simply enjoy the beauty of the world? The day is given you not for a day of restraint, but for a holiday; you were not made for it, to spend it in a particular way, but it was made for you, to spend in the way you find most for your advantage.

The religious character of the day may be trusted to take care of itself; it needs no civil laws nor any intervention of the magistrate to secure it. This was the case with the weekly rest before the rise of Sabbatarianism, and it will be the case again when Sabbatarianism has ceased to afflict mankind. Men turn naturally to religion when their thoughts are free; it is natural to them to assemble together, and they will not fail to do so whenever religious ordinances are provided in which they can intelligently take part. In countries where a great part of the population has ceased to go to church, the reason is not that they hold too loose a view of the Sabbath law, but that the church from lack of zeal or from lack of intellectual courage, has failed to command the sympathy of the intelligent population. There is no more beautiful spectacle anywhere to be seen, there is no influence that refreshes and comforts the spirit more gently, no agency that more surely brings to the wounded and oppressed heart the healing touch of sympathy and enthusiasm, than the public worship of God. That is a cold statement; the assurances and encouragements that worship brings are more than those of human fellowship alone; and to suppose that the church should provide services in which the deep needs of the human soul are met, and in which neither the sense of beauty nor the love of truth need be offended, but that such services should be forsaken of worshippers because people have changed their views of the obligation of Sunday, is to suppose an impossibility.

The institution of the seventh day's rest will yet prove far more useful to this country than it has hitherto been allowed to be. That earnestness of character and that reverence for the divine commands, which have made our Sundays gloomy and difficult to spend, will not desert us though we should cease to be specially in awe of that day of the week, and will find expression on that day even when it is dedicated more than it is now to the spirit of humanity and freedom.

THE FIFTH COMMANDMENT.

Honour thy father and thy mother; that thy days may be long upon the land which the Lord thy God giveth thee.

This, the apostle Paul says, is the first commandment with promise. It enjoins obedience to parents, and promises long life to those who obey their parents. So at least the promise is commonly interpreted: it is thought to hold out the expectation that if a man honour his parents he will live a longer life than he otherwise would: Respect to this commandment is thought to carry with it the assurance of individual longevity.

It is difficult to understand such a promise. The blessing promised must surely have some natural connection with the virtue enjoined: that is the way with all God's rewards, they are the natural consequences of keeping his commandments. But it is hard to see what necessary connection there is between honouring our parents and living threescore and ten or fourscore years.

The promise must surely have a wider meaning than this interpretation allows to it. Indeed we see at once that it is not addressed to individuals but to a people. The land of promise was not given to individuals but to the Jewish nation. They are here told of one essential condition of their keeping it and enjoying in it a quiet and peaceful national existence. If they are to dwell quietly in the land, if their state is to have a firm basis and continue from age to age free from revolution and decay, there must be respect to parents, children must honour their father and mother. And if the promise points to national continuance as well as to the longevity of individuals, then it is not a promise chosen at random: the keeping of the commandment has a natural tendency to bring about the promised blessing. The state in which parents are honoured and obeyed will naturally be stable and secure, and the promise will be fulfilled to individuals too, because life will be safe in it.

That this is really the case a very little consideration is enough to show. What is it that makes any state strong and stable, that saves it from revolution and civil war, and procures for it the respect of other states? It is the loyalty of its citizens, the obedience they yield to the laws and the government, their habits of self-restraint and self-denial for the public good, their reverence for the constitution under which they live, their determination to uphold the authority of the state against the lawlessness and the caprice of parties and of individuals. A state cannot be strong in which the laws are not willingly obeyed, or in which there either is no central authority capable of ruling, or that authority is constantly disregarded. Should the doctrine unhappily prevail which is now put forward even in influential quarters, that people are not bound to obey laws which they find very inconvenient, or of which they say that they disapprove, or should it be possible for any class which dislikes the fulfilment of its legal obligations, to band itself together in order to repudiate its lawful duties or fraudulently to evade them, there government is at an end, and the country which tolerates such doctrines and practices has no prospect before it but civil war with the probable issue of a military despotism. There can be no order or security and consequently there can be no freedom, when the different classes and members of the state do not willingly accept the positions they occupy in the state, and perform the duties they owe to it. And thus in order that the state may be strong its citizens must be trained in certain necessary virtues; they must have learned the habits of respect for authority, of obedience to law, of self-denial, of consideration for the interests and claims of others.

In what school are the citizens to be trained in these all-important habits? Where, and at what part of their lives, are they to learn to reverence authority, to keep the law, to curb their own caprices and desires? It will be too late to learn these lessons when they attain the rights and responsibility of citizenship, if they have not been learning them before. Nor can the school teach them if it is opposed by an earlier and deeper influence. These things must be learned in the family. The father and mother are to their children the first representatives of all authority and law. The family is the first community in which the child finds himself living with others whose wishes and interests he must respect. His father and mother are the sovereign rulers, his brothers and sisters are the fellow-subjects, in that little community. In the family accordingly the habits must be formed which in later life make men useful citizens who add strength to the state. If the family is what it should be, if the government is strong there, if the laws there are clear and firmly maintained, if lessons of obedience and self-control are taught there, the state will be provided with a race of good citizens who will reverence the law and count the prosperity of the nation of more importance than their own, and who will live together in peace. Where the institution of the family is falling into decay, so that children grow up wilful and undisciplined and bent on nothing but on their own pleasures and on having their own way, there the state will tend to be insecure, so that it will be subject to frequent changes and disturbances, and will invite the attacks of its enemies. The family is the nursery of the state. Sound, healthy, simple, religious family life, the maintenance of the institution of the family in vigour and piety, is the very first social condition of national well-being.

Such is the first commandment of the second table of the Decalogue, and the others are in spirit like it. The great principles of spiritual religion once laid down in the first table, religion hastens to identify itself with the fundamental principles and institutions of civilisation. Here God is not claiming anything for himself, he is asking for no sacrifices or offerings; no religious rites are ordained, there is no mention of the temple or the priesthood. God appears not as one who sets up rival demands to those of the earthly state, not as one who seeks to draw men away from the service of the State to what might be deemed a more sacred service. He appears, on the contrary, as the founder of the State, as the source and the upholder of civil order and of the freedom which that order guarantees, as the giver of the laws on which society reposes. The great principles of civilised society appear as divine commands, as belonging to the number of the most solemn and most important laws which God addresses to man. Society is thus represented to the eyes of man as a divine work: the laws of society are divine laws; the fabric of society is not a result of chance or of arbitrary human arrangement; the marriage bond, the family tie, the institution of property, the administration of justice, these are all to be regarded as divine institutions, given to man for his benefit, and to be held sacred and inviolable. Wherever these institutions prevail —and they prevail wherever man is civilised —the pious mind will readily agree to the claim which the Decalogue makes for them of a sacred origin. Whatever view be taken of the formation of the Decalogue, or even omitting all reference to the Decalogue, the pious and reasonable mind will be inclined to recognise in the essential conditions of society a divine ordinance, to which man ought to submit as he submits to the climate he lives in, which he need not think of altering, from which he should not desire to escape. And should it appear in the sifting critical process to which all the arrangements of human life are and ought to be subjected, that these institutions could not have been other than they are, that man never could have prospered in the world nor attained to civilization with any other institutions than these, then the pious and reasonable mind will be greatly strengthened in the view it is naturally inclined to take, and will declare that the Decalogue is beyond all question right, when it says that God gave man these laws, and that his authority upholds and will always continue to uphold them.

The family like all other human institutions has had its history. It did not appear perfect all at once, but is the result of a long process of development. Even in the Old Testament we have abundant evidence of a state of society in which the family as we know it, could not be said to exist. The Fifth Commandment presupposes that monogamy is the practice of society: in a society where polygamy prevails the parents are not in a position to claim that undoubted obedience and respect which the commandment exacts for them. In the earlier ages of Israel the mother could not have been placed by the side of the father as entitled to the same honour with him from the children of the family. True family life cannot exist, with its thorough training and cultivation of character, if the necessary preparation has not been made for it in a civilized institution of marriage.

And what is thus true on a large scale is beyond doubt true also in individual cases. The success of the family as a school of thrift and order and a nursery of good citizens, depends on the conditions on which it is formed at the outset. The parents evidently have to prepare a place in which the children can be reasonably expected to practise obedience. The children cannot keep the fifth commandment until the parents have first made it possible for them to do so. Children will grow up on the whole what their parents make them; should they grow up self-willed, impatient of authority, and bent on nothing but their own pleasure, it must be in great part the parents' fault.

We leave it to the next discourse to speak of the duty children owe to their parents, and speak now of the duty of parents to their children. The fifth commandment would not be properly expounded if the first conditions of sound family life, which depend on the parents, were not insisted on. The family is founded on the marriage tie, and those children will keep this commandment most naturally, whose parents have made a real marriage. A sound family life can only spring out of a true union of the parents. When a man and woman can declare that they believe it to be a part of the eternal fitness of things that they should be united, then their marriage may be said to be not of the will of the flesh nor of the will of man but of God, and then the true authority exists which the children will cheerfully obey. Those who are thus united rule over their children by divine right; the higher power which made them one, commissions them its representatives as the heads of the family. There is no source of parental authority half so profound or so unfailing as this. A true union of the parents will prevent the appearance of that which most of all makes obedience difficult, namely the division of the authority to which it is due. Where the father and mother do not present to their children a united front, their influence is wasted, and a painful conflict of duties arises in their children's minds, since they cannot cleave to the one without despising the other. If the fifth commandment is to be obeyed, father and mother must be in harmony; there must be no appeal from the one to the other; the children must feel that what their father says their mother says too, that what their mother asks their father asks too, and will exact if called to do so.

And love will find the best solutions of the various educational difficulties as they arise. One of these which is constantly recurring is how to uphold the rule of justice in the family and yet remember mercy, how to combine strictness with indulgence. If children are not accustomed to the rule of laws they must not break, they will grow up self-indulgent and weak in will; if their childhood is not bright and sunny, they will grow up timid, and the powers they naturally possess may never be developed. On the one hand the family must have laws, and obedience to these laws must be exacted; children must learn, and learn early, to do what they are bid, and to consider the wishes and feelings of others. And to this end rules must be set up which the children are on no account to transgress. But on the other hand a cast-iron system, enforced on every occasion and in spite of whatever friction may arise, is quite out of place in a circle, where all should grow up free and happy. Children are not pieces of wood to be cut to a pattern with rule and square: they are living growths which must be studied, humoured and fostered. The family is not to be governed by a code, but by a government which sympathises with its subjects, and has no aim but to secure their welfare and happiness. And this government, if it is wise, will be looking forward to the time when it will cease to govern, and will not drill its subjects too much nor allow them to lean too much on authority, so that when the time comes for them to act alone, they may be found fit for liberty.

The difficulty of combining firmness and indulgence in the management of children, is one which must be dealt with in each case separately; no fixed rules can be given with regard to it; it cannot be overcome successfully without study and taking trouble. Parents may shirk it in various ways. They may set up the system of force and declare their own will to be an absolute law which is to be carried out in all instances; this plan will spoil their children very effectually in one way. Or they may shirk the difficulty by letting their children do what they like, purchasing their obedience when it must be had, with bribes, and giving way at the sight of their tears; and thus spoil them very effectually in another way. Those who desire that their children should be obedient and yet happy and free, must study the case they have to deal with, and must be prepared to take trouble. The pains they take, the never-wearying labour of love, will gain its object, and will make the memory of home a never-failing fountain of strength and happiness to their children throughout their lives.

One thing more is clear and must be said before concluding. The rules you set up for your household, you must show that you yourself reverence and observe. Parents who would have their children respect their authority, must show them that it springs from a higher source than their own will. And these rules must be reasonable and wise, and such as recommend themselves by their own force. Your children will reverence only that to which they see that you yourself are looking up. You must shew them that you too are living in obedience to a law given from above. You must banish caprice and arbitrariness from your dealings with them: you must treat them all alike. You must not treat them as playthings, but as beings equally important with yourself. You must teach them to look up to the one great source of all authority and law, and encourage them to live as you yourself do, as in God's eye and engaged in his service. Teach them that in obeying you they are obeying not you only but God; and let your treatment of them and the demands you make upon them, be such as agree with such a claim; and they will not fail to honour their father and mother, nor as long as they live, to bless the names of those who made their childhood and youth so sweet and holy and secure.

THE FIFTH COMMANDMENT.

SECOND DISCOURSE.

Honour thy father and thy mother.

IMMEDIATELY after the commandments which speak of man's duty to God, comes this one which speaks of his duty to his father and mother, who are the first representatives of God to him upon the earth. This commandment precedes those which forbid murder and theft; the duty it enjoins comes earlier in point of time than those we owe to our neighbours. The man who keeps this commandment well, will be less apt to transgress those which come after it. He who honours his parents will form habits of self-control and of consideration for others, which will be a safeguard to him in other directions. If violent impulses are curbed here, they will be more likely to be curbed in all the parts of life. The man who has been a good son will be most likely to prove a good neighbour, a good husband, a good governor of his own desires. The catechisms of the churches in England and Scotland make this commandment extend to a number of matters which it does not mention, and interpret it as enjoining loyalty to the Queen, and respectful and dutiful conduct to our superiors, inferiors, and equals, in society. The compilers of these catechisms thought the ten commandments contained the whole of human duty, and made them embrace entire provinces of conduct. With regard to the fifth commandment, the view they took was undoubtedly true. It does not mention civil rulers, or teachers, or masters, or servants; but he who fails in his duties to his parents, will fail in his duties towards other persons too. The virtues children learn to practise in the family are the same virtues which are necessary for citizens in the state, for members of the Church, and for those who would discharge aright social observances and courtesies.

To honour one's parents includes obeying them, but it includes something more. It suggests that "rising up before the hoary head" which the proverb enjoins, and which we feel to be so natural and becoming. Parents ought to receive such deference as is due to those of a higher rank, their wishes and opinions should be attentively considered, their tastes should be consulted. To treat them with undue familiarity may be a worse transgression of the commandment than to neglect some of their injunctions. To treat parents with disrespect, the Bible regards as the worst sin against them; indeed, it was a sin which among the Jews was to be visited, in certain cases, with the penalty of death. The story of the treatment of Noah by his unworthy son, was an example of what was most repugnant to Jewish sentiment; and the Proverbs tell us what the Jewish mind conceived to be the proper attitude which a son ought to take up towards his parents: "My son, keep thy father's commandment and forsake not the law of thy mother. Where thou goest it shall lead thee: when thou sleepest it shall keep thee: when thou awakest it shall talk with thee."

We need no proof that what this commandment enjoins is right. We look with pity on those tribes of men among whom parents are no longer cared for when they grow weak and old, and the helpless father is left by his children to a solitary death; these tribes have not yet attained to true humanity; some of the tenderest and noblest aspects of our nature are not known to them. The conduct of Goneril and Regan we instinctively regard with abhorrence; if there ever was a time when the difference between their conduct and that of Cordelia would not have been understood, that must have been a savage time, when man had not yet put on his true nature. The duty this commandment enforces is so natural that no argument can add to its sacredness. The Decalogue places it first among the duties we owe to our fellow-creatures, and proclaims it without any qualification or reserve. The sixth commandment offers no proof that murder is wrong. The fifth offers no proof that it is right to honour our parents. That is a law with regard to which there is no doubt: a law which, beyond all doubt or question, is written on the heart.

Indeed the breach of this commandment is more unnatural, more repugnant to every healthy sentiment than that of any of the others. The language we address to children in speaking of their duty, is language which stirs tender feelings in every breast. "Think, we say, of all your parents have done for you since you came into the world. They cared for you, watched over you, worked for you, when you could give them no thanks, nor reward them in any way. How ill off you would be without them, and when you think of the sorrow it will be to you some day, perhaps, to lose them, are you not determined to give them all the respect and affection you can while they are still with you? The instinctive partiality they feel for you, you will never find again in any one in this world; and would it not be an intolerable thought that when this priceless affection was lavished upon you, you repaid it with indifference? The time will come for you also when old age and failing strength will overtake you; and as you desire to find helpers and comforters when you need them, see that you help and comfort those who need them now." But all these considerations and a hundred more which we might urge, will help little in the case of those who do not feel their duty to their parents without them. God does not speak to us about our father and mother in any such roundabout fashion. He says plainly and simply, as a matter regarding which there can be no doubt, which admits of no argument, *Honour thy father and thy mother.* He whose conscience does not tell him at once that he ought to do this, that this is right, will not be much affected by any arguments to prove it.

The commandment is quite absolute, quite unconditional. It does not say, honour your parents if you consider that they are kind to you, or if they have cultivated tastes and opinions, or if they are persons of good standing who are generally looked up to. Whatever they are in these and in similar respects, to you they must be more than any other people in the world, for you there is no choice but to look up to them and cherish them; to you they fill a place which no others can ever occupy, on you they have a claim which no others can have. The treatment you give them will dwell in your memory, will form the subject of your wayside thoughts, and fill you with light or else with darkness as long as you live. It is God's will that you should see in them those who were his first representatives to you. As you fear God and look for his favour, you are bound to reverence and honour them.

There comes a time, however, to many young people whose parents are happily spared to them, when the entire and unquestioning deference paid at first quite naturally, becomes no longer possible. A child whose father and mother are united in their counsels, regards them as supreme, and never dreams that they may be wrong, or that there are any better people in the world. Nor need much importance be attached to the child's discovery that his parents do not know everything. He comes home from school with dates or rules of grammar of which his mother if she ever knew them, has been long forgetful: but to a healthy child this will make little difference. If he sees that she rejoices in his progress and is anxious that he should learn more and more, his advance in learning will not divide him from her. But the time inevitably comes in the course of nature when children in some respects outgrow their parents. They form interests and affections which must be satisfied elsewhere than at home. Perhaps they come to hold views for which the home has little sympathy. Their own wings have grown, and they can no longer depend upon their parents for the food of their minds and spirits. These things must be. Parents cannot expect to keep their children to themselves. The human race is their mother too, and has a thousand things to tell them that their immediate parents do not know.

But this does not bring the obligation of the fifth commandment to an end. Nothing can ever do so. However far we wander from the views on which our childhood was nourished, and whatever limitations we discover in the character of our parents, their claim upon us can never be effaced. We can never cease to be their children, and to owe them honour and affection. However we cultivate ourselves, and whatever ties we form apart from our parents, how good it is for us to go back to the attitude of little children, to put on again the unquestioning deference which used to be so natural, to clothe ourselves again in the spirit of childhood and look up with gratitude and reverence to those who first loved us and sheltered us! Happy those who still enjoy such opportunities!

There are some things, Christ tells us, which we must not do even for our parents' sake. The gospels say many strong things about the duty which may arise to cast off the bonds of family. When a new religion is being launched in the world, great sacrifices are required of those who offer themselves as its missionaries. Jesus himself forsook his mother and his family, and turned coldly away from them when he thought they were seeking to obstruct his enterprise. He that loveth father or mother more than me, he said, is not worthy of me.

It is always possible that such difficulties may reappear. It is God's will that we should honour our parents, but cases may arise in which we feel that God is calling us to a course of duty in which we cannot obey them nor please them. Duty may still appear sometimes bearing not peace, but a sword. A man may feel himself called to perform a duty to society by taking up a part of which his parents disapprove, or by devoting himself to a different profession from that which they marked out for him. Or he may have contracted obligations to others which he cannot repudiate without dishonour, and cannot fulfil without causing his parents great pain. Such cases must be exceptional, and we should not think lightly that such a thing has happened to us. He who finds that he cannot take his parents into his confidence should for a time distrust himself and think that the path which leads him away from them, cannot be the right path. And when difficulties arise we should not press matters, but should see what time and temper can do to remove them. When a real conflict of duties appears and a choice must be made between two courses, each of them hard, we must of course do the duty which we are convinced is the higher of the two, and the more plainly laid upon us by God.

But Christ who thus spoke of the duty which might lead a man to forsake his father and mother, spoke also with incomparable force of the natural duty which lies upon all men to do for their father and mother all they can. A man cannot be excused, he taught, who prefers to the natural duty of maintaining his parents some piece of fantastic religious devotion. A man should give up his own tastes and fancies, and should rather retrench his liberality to the church than fail to fulfil this venerable obligation which God has imposed on all men. The duty men owe to their parents is set forth in that chapter as one which can never be out of date, and which no human fashion can be allowed to set aside.

THE SIXTH COMMANDMENT.

Thou shalt not kill.

READING the historical books of the Old Testament, one might be inclined to say that reverence for human life was not a virtue on which the Jews could pride themselves, and that in this important particular, they were little advanced in civilization. In the early monarchy, the crime of assassination was terribly common. Some of the great heroes of Jewish religion were notable inciters to, or perpetrators of, murder and massacre; Samuel, David, Jehu, and Elijah, were all distinguished in this way. The prophet Hosea looked back with horror on the massacres of Jehu; in the rational and humane religion of the prophets a much higher value was attached to human life. But when a narrower religious spirit again laid hold of the Jews after the exile, human life came to be rated more cheaply, and was held less sacred than the ritual observance of the priestly law. The book of Joshua, a work of a late period, represented the early wars of the Jews, wars in which they are said to have been led by Jehovah himself, as having been extremely cruel and bloody, and generally aimed at the extermination of their enemies. And some of the laws belonging to this later period, though they can scarcely have been generally acted on, have a sanguinary tone, and denounce capital punishment against a number of offences, some of them by no means offences of the first magnitude, such as gathering sticks on the Sabbath day, or putting one's foot within a sacred enclosure, or consulting a wizard. This depreciation of the value of human life, though in many instances it appears as dictated by God himself, as a part of the religious system he had set up, is a sign of a decline in civilization among the Jews; and proves that the spirit of the sixth commandment, a law so necessary to the existence of security and freedom, had not perfectly taken possession of their minds.

What is forbidden in this commandment is an act of impatience, of passion, of blind intolerance.

We may study it on a small scale in children. A child seeing an insect it does not know or is afraid of, at once calls out for its destruction, and seeks to put an end to it, to thrust it out of sight. In the same way men at a low stage of advancement deal with human beings who are obnoxious to them, with those who have crossed their plans, or who have done them an injury, or who entertain objectionable opinions. It may have occurred to many of us with regard to persons who are an obstacle to us, or who pursue what we consider a reprehensible line of conduct, that it would be better if they were out of the way, and altogether ceased from troubling. This is the root-thought of murder, the wish that some one were removed. This wish felt in a stronger degree by a nature less under the bonds of education and custom than is commonly the case in our day, is what makes murderers. They make their wish their law, and carry it out with their own hands.

In an age when institutions were less settled than they are now, and when men had to defend their lives and property without any police or magistrates to help them, murder could not be very rare.

And even in a more settled society it may often appear that the simplest and easiest plan to take with offenders of various kinds, was simply to put them out of the way, to kill them. If a man had done you an injury, or if he belonged to a class you thought you had good reason to hate, or if he possessed something you wanted but could not get while he was there, what so natural as to remove the obstruction from your path? Even religion has often felt and acted in this way. If a man followed the wrong religion and worshipped the wrong God in a country, what plan could go so well to the root of such an evil and extirpate idolatry from the land, as simply to extirpate the idolaters? So Elijah hurried the priests of Baal down to the brook Jabbok and slew them there. It did not occur to him to think of them as brother men, as men who might be converted to the true worship and live useful lives afterwards; he must take the shortest way. So also the Inquisition treated the Protestant heretics in Spain and Holland in the sixteenth century; heretics could not be allowed to live; they had no rights, they were simply to be got out of the way as expeditiously as possible.

Now it is an essential condition of society that human life should be regarded as sacred and inviolable. Where human life is not secure, no useful industry can flourish, and the advantages which flow from the co-operation of the various members of the state cannot be enjoyed. The passionate and violent have a fatal advantage over the peaceable and industrious; the worst are strongest, the wise and reasonable can effect nothing, and there is no liberty for any one. The growth of the value attached to human life is an accurate index of the increase of civilisation with all its attendant blessings.

The Sixth Commandment is an edict, when we consider it attentively, of astonishing simplicity and comprehensiveness. It is expressed in such absolute terms as to give it a universal scope, and could not be received by any people without suggesting reflection as to the relation between the Legislator and the life He protects so solemnly, and as to the consequent relation of men to each other. Like the other commandments it derives weight from its brevity; it speaks of no exceptions, and thus tends to make these as few as possible. It says nothing of the distinction between Jew and Gentile, and the Jew is thus given to understand that it shelters the Gentile as well as his brother Jew. It declares human life as such to be a sacred thing with which man dare not meddle, a thing mysterious and infinite, to be left by us where God has placed it. It reminds us of that most broad and Catholic account which the book of Genesis gives of the creation of man, where we read that God made man in his own image and breathed into his nostrils the breath of life, and where we find as we read further, that the race thus highly favoured at their birth were not special favourites of heaven, while others were descended from a meaner origin, but the stem from which all the families of the earth alike proceeded. If all men have a common origin and all alike derive their breath from the highest source, then it is clear that the murder of any man, whatever race he belongs to and whatever his character or history, is an act which cannot be unobserved by God, and that the doing of such an act without the most invincible necessity is a terrible crime. It is an offence against the whole human family; for all mankind are kindred to the slain; it is a crime against our own family, for he came of our own stock; it is a crime against our own nature, for his nature was the same as ours, it came from the same source, and was composed of the same elements. It is an act which neither passion nor religious zeal, neither ancestral custom nor the rules of any society men may belong to, can possibly excuse. The law which forbids it is a law written on human nature from the first, and never to be expunged or tampered with in favour of any institution or any interest of man.

That this law and the spirit which dictated it, cannot have been very closely present to the minds of the Jewish people at some parts of their history, or to the minds of some of their legislators, we have already seen. But the simple and early Jewish laws with regard to murder show the idea which the sixth commandment expresses to have been indigenous in the Jewish race; and we can trace in the Bible how, as the Jews came to hold deeper ideas as to the value of human life, a more humane character was also imparted to their laws. A word on this subject may show us how the spirit of the sixth commandment must act on the laws and the temper of a nation.

With other Eastern tribes the early Hebrews considered murder to be a crime for which nothing could atone but the death of the murderer. The murderer they considered to have become the enemy of the human race. "He who slayeth a soul," the Koran says, "shall be as if he had slain all mankind." And Cain says after the murder of Abel, "Whosoever findeth me shall slay me." Nor was it only man who cried for vengeance on the slayer. The ground which had been compelled to drink innocent blood became a partaker of the crime, but not a willing partaker. The land became the enemy of the slayer, and cried out to be purified from the stain it had unwillingly contracted. (Numbers, xxxv. 33).

To these deep and powerful sentiments effect was given among the Hebrews and other peoples by the institution of blood-revenge. The next of kin to the murdered person became his avenger, an office in which public sympathy supported him. In the absence of any regular machinery of justice the avenger represented the public, and executed the sentence which ancient usage approved of. If the avenger died, his heir inherited this obligation.

The Jewish law recognises the institution of blood-revenge as a mode of the execution of justice, and only seeks to regulate it. The principal change introduced by the law on the older practice consisted in the distinction which was now drawn between wilful murder and unintentional manslaughter. The slayer formerly forfeited his life to the avenger, whether his act had been a deliberate murder or the result of an accident; but the law while leaving the practice unchanged for the former case, provided a means of escape for the slayer in the latter, by instituting cities of refuge, where on proving that the shedding of blood for which he was pursued by the avenger, had not been malicious but accidental, he should enjoy protection.

There thus appears on the part of the Jewish legislation, a desire to correct the old superstitious notion that one violent death must in every case be followed by another. A more humane and reasonable spirit introduces a distinction between the slayer, whose life is morally forfeited, and the other, whose act does not make him an enemy of mankind. One who has been unfortunate enough to bring about the death of a fellow-creature without intending it, is not to be sacrificed to a punctilio of superstition or to private revenge. Human life is too sacred to be dealt with in such a way. And so while the old safeguards are kept up as against the murderer, a door of escape is opened to the unfortunate homicide.

This example shows in a very apposite way the true bearing of the sixth commandment on legislation. A state which desires to uphold that commandment must itself set the example of reverence for human life, by reducing as far as possible the number of the offences to which it affixes the penalty of death. No offenders must be put to death but those whose crimes mark them as dangerous to the lives of their fellow-citizens, or to the existence of the state. People must not be put to death for theft or forgery, nor for any offence which can be adequately discouraged otherwise. Human beings must not be put to death for ecclesiastical offences, or for the opinions which they hold. Thus society attests its regard for the sacredness of human life. But at the same time society retains the right to deal in the only adequate way with those who have committed murder. No society can give up the right to defend its own existence in this way and in other ways, such as the execution of traitors and the waging of war, which may involve the sacrifice of many lives. Society is greater than the individual, and when occasion arises, the existence of the individual must be sacrificed, that that of the society may continue.

But with these limitations, the sixth commandment is a great edict of toleration for all who are living in the world. It proclaims toleration for the unpopular, for evil-doers, for the holders of strange opinions, for the followers of new courses and policies. People are not to be treated as passion might dictate, because they are disliked by their neighbours, nor because they have committed some offence, if it can be otherwise dealt with, nor because their aims are ever so distasteful. Human life is a sacred thing, a thing never to be violated at man's caprice, or brushed aside by his passion. When God bids a man live on the earth, that divine behest must be obeyed, and the man allowed to live out his span. The right of depriving others of their existence, is a right that does not belong to any man. Every one who is born into the world is to be tolerated there.

As expounded by our Lord Jesus Christ the commandment requires much more than this. It forbids not only the act of murder, but the feelings from which murder ultimately springs, and even such expression of these feelings as stops far short of bloodshed. It forbids us to be angry with our brother, or to hurl opprobrious epithets at him. This explanation makes the commandment carry far indeed, and yet the principle of tolerating all men on the earth's surface being once set up, could not stop short at the mere concession of their right to exist. If life is guaranteed to them surely it is for the sake of what they are to do in it, and they must be allowed not only to breathe but to speak and act as they are fitted to do, and to show forth to the world what is in them. It would be but a questionable boon, a poor toleration, only half the keeping of the commandment, to make life sacred but to refuse liberty. And as the commandment was in old times a check on wildness and passion and fanaticism, training a rude people to give up the practice of assassination, and the bigot to restrain his persecuting instinct, so its spirit is still at work where pure religion lives, teaching men to take a just view even of the acts and the character of their adversaries, and to curb within their breasts the old Adam of hatred and intolerance. Confronted with those whose character we cannot admire, whose sentiments are hateful to us, whose aims appear to us doubtful or mischievous, we are yet led by the spirit of these venerable words to repress our impatience, and to concede to others the free exercise of their abilities and opportunities. God has placed us men all together in this world with widely different characters and tendencies, and with eager desires and interests which in many ways bring us into conflict with each other. We may often wish, we can scarcely refrain from wishing, that he had made the world less mixed, that some of its contrasts were less glaring, some of its conflicts less terrible. But we must let the mixture work as he intended; while doing all we can for what we consider the good cause, we must allow to others the same freedom which we claim for ourselves. We must cultivate a spirit of fairness and justice towards all our fellow-creatures with whom we have to do, and by every means seek to escape out of the realm of violence into the realm of reason. God is not the author of physical life alone, but also of the life of the mind in all its manifold forms; this life also which he gave he commands us to respect, showing our faith in him and our reverence for his work by extending to all his creatures equal consideration and fair play.

THE SEVENTH COMMANDMENT.

Thou shalt not commit adultery.

THE Old Testament contains many traces of a growth in the marriage customs of the Hebrews, from practices which we should consider singular and barbarous, to the monogamy which Christianity inherited from Judaism and has always upheld. That the early Hebrews had not attained to the conception of marriage as a lifelong union upon equal terms of one man and one woman, a glance at the histories of the Old Testament will show: and the marriage laws of the Pentateuch testify to the same effect. It has recently been shown that the family of tribes to which Israel belonged practised in early times that kind of marriage which causes the family to trace its descent to the mother rather than to the father, and that traces of this practice are to be found in the expressions, and to a small extent also in the ideas, of the Old Testament. At the period when the history of Israel dawns, however, the more civilised practice of descent in the male line had quite established itself. The children belonged to the father, and were brought up under his roof. But he was not limited to one wife; he might if he chose have two or even more. He was not allowed to marry within certain degrees of relationship, and he was forbidden to have a mother and daughter, or two sisters, for his wives at the same time; but the law did not limit the number of his wives. Accordingly we see the kings of Israel, who are also the heads of the national religion, surround themselves with many wives; and when Nathan comes to David to rebuke him in the matter of Bathsheba, all he says is that the king who had so many wives already, and might if he had chosen have had more, has appropriated the wife of a man who had only one. And the objection made to the multitudinous wives of Solomon, is that he selected them from the Canaanite tribes, with whom the Israelites were forbidden to intermarry, and suffered them to turn away his heart from the national religion. The polygamy which the kings thus practised, was not forbidden to their subjects, and was not regarded by them as wrong. The patriarchs, the great models of Jewish religion, were not restricted to monogamy; and while the marriage laws remained as they are in the book of Leviticus, polygamy was legal, and was only condemned, if at all, by the gradual refinement of public opinion. We are able to trace the growth of public opinion in this direction. In the book of Deuteronomy, which belongs to the age of Josiah, it is enjoined upon the king not to multiply his wives; but before this time monogamy had come to be the general practice in Israel, though instances of a man's having two wives are recorded without any remark. The laws regulating polygamy remained on the statute-book, but polygamy as a practice disappeared. In the Proverbs no other notion of marriage appears, but that which belongs to civilisation. The view of marriage which came to prevail among the Jews, is set forth in a picture in the history of the creation. Adam and Eve are the typical wedded pair, in whom the true wedded state, the marriage for which man was made, is to be seen.

We thus see that the earlier the seventh commandment is placed in the history of Israel, the more widely do the circumstances to which it was addressed, differ from those in which we live. The promulgation of it can scarcely belong to an age in which a strictly monogamous institution of marriage prevailed. We must conceive it to have been addressed at first to people who did not think of marriage just as we do, and therefore to have been aimed at somewhat different offences from those which we now regard as sins against the marriage tie. All that it seeks to protect in fact, is the right of the husband, and the sacredness of his household. It did not when first given, forbid irregularities between unmarried people; and it could not forbid a man's attentions to a woman whom he might add, if he chose, to the number of his wives. All it forbad was an attack upon his neighbour's domestic peace. "Thou shalt not covet thy neighbour's wife" forbids the lust of which this commandment forbids the indulgence. The law contains no appeal to the general sentiment of reverence for woman, nor to the principle of personal temperance and self-respect; it only forbids the wife to be untrue to her husband, and the neighbour to infringe upon the rights of a neighbour.

But a divine law has such virtue that it can elevate and purify the institutions with which it is connected. A law accepted as divine gathers a depth and a range of application, not contemplated by those who first promulgated it. The mind sees in it more than a mere police regulation, finds ever new motives for keeping it, and seeks to read in it the ordinance of nature. As its meaning is more deeply apprehended, the deficiences of the institution in which it is set forth, are successively revealed. And religion, such religion, at least, as seeks its sphere, like that of Moses and the prophets, in the simple and reasonable duties of life, is thus the mainspring of the growth of civilization. Commandments so short and simple as those of the Decalogue, contain within themselves the germ of an infinite social advancement. Rude as the customs are to which they bear reference at first, yet the recognition in these rude customs of sacred, God-appointed duties, is a guarantee that the customs will themselves grow purer. Reflection on the divine law cannot fail to bring about an improvement in the institution. And so it happens that by regarding their early marriage customs with reverence, and treating a sin against the marriage tie as a sin against God, the Jews advanced from those ruder practices of which we have spoken, to that institution of marriage which the civilised world now possesses. Belonging to the East, in which the position of woman was notoriously a low one, they yet attained a more civilised institution of marriage, and a higher view of the nature of woman, than did Greece and Rome. So true is it that to those who are faithful in small things more will be given. A true religious principle faithfully followed out will by degrees transform even the most defective institutions, and will ultimately lead to those which are according to reason, and fitted to prove permanently suitable to human nature.

That the institution of marriage which came at last to prevail among the Jews, and which now prevails in all Christian lands, is the most suitable and natural to man, and may be regarded as that for which man was made, and which the divine law, the law of his own constitution, imposes upon him, there is not perhaps any great need to prove. Few will question that the Bible is right in transferring this, the ultimate result of age-long progress in this matter, to the beginning of man's life upon the globe, and representing the union of one man and one woman as a divine institution, and as the arrangement which is intrinsically fit and right for man. Some students, it is true, have reached a different conclusion. Surveying the strange diversity of marriage customs in various ages and lands, many of which demand much less self-restraint than that under which we live, and seeing in the frequent breaches of the law among ourselves, a tendency to revert to earlier practices, some have argued that the lower type of the relations of the sexes is the more natural, and that were it not for certain incidental disadvantages, a return to it might be desirable. But surely this is to consult the feet of the human race on a question which only its head is competent to answer. It is likely that the state which is most suitable to man is that to which his manifold experiments have at last conducted him. Surely the institution which alone has made modern life possible, which has brought to bear on human life purifying and refining influences which were never felt in the ancient world, is the matured fruit of human growth in this direction, a fruit to be jealously guarded, and never exchanged even in thought for the usages of earlier and coarser times.

The reasons for upholding the present ordinance of marriage, and for regarding it as by far the most suitable and natural to man, and therefore possessing the divine sanction, are many and of immeasurable weight. We can do little more than enumerate the more important of them.

1. No other system does justice to the nature of woman as a reasonable and immortal being. To regard woman as a mere instrument or property, or as the means for an end, is fatally to degrade her. She has a right to be regarded as of equal importance with man, and in marriage her interest must be consulted to an equal degree with his. Her freedom and happiness must be secured, if she is to grow into that which she is fitted to become, and

this can only be done by making her the equal head of the house along with her husband.

2. It is only by such a pure and simple marriage custom as we possess, that a true family is possible. In speaking of the fourth commandment we have already insisted upon this. Children who do not look up to father and mother as one joint authority, start in life under heavy disadvantages. To the children of Jacob the fifth commandment could not appear so naturally binding as it now does, nor to the children of Elkanah, nor to the sons of David. It is only the united and co-ordinate authority of one man and one woman, that can make the family a real school of obedience and reverence for the children, and no one can calculate how much society would lose if no such school existed, or if its laws were weakened.

3. No other system is so favourable to romance. The old tales would not be half so charming if they concluded with any other words than the familiar ones, that the hero and heroine, who had gone through so much for each others' sake, "lived happily together ever after." Where marriage is not regarded as a lifelong union, woman

cannot be regarded with so much reverence, and courtship must have less of that feeling of awe which it brings to the best men, and which belongs to it, if it is the beginning of a union which is indissoluble and which has infinite issues. How greatly life must lose in depth and interest, not only for individuals but for the whole population of a country, when women are not regarded with reverence, and romantic courtship is not believed in, a slight acquaintance with French fiction may convince us.

It is a great mistake, therefore, to speak of marriage as it exists among us, as a mere decent external conventionality. It is true that the essence of marriage lies under the surface, and that where there is no union of hearts, no heavenly leading of man and woman to each other, the outward tie has little true meaning. But if the idea of marriage is greater than the institution, the institution on the other hand lends support to the idea, and it is something to be proud of and to guard with jealous care, that we possess a marriage institution, which in outward respects secures woman's position as man's equal helpmate, and declares the union of the two to be lifelong. In upholding the marriage bond as presently existing among us, we are not defending a mere conventionality; we are pleading that the advance which the human race has won in securing the position of woman, should not be surrendered; we are pleading for the protection of woman from those who do not sufficiently reverence her; we are pleading for the children of the state, that they may continue to enjoy the care of a father and a mother. Only those who would be content to see woman sink below her present position, can see with equanimity the obligation of marriage set at naught, or forms of indulgence practised which involve the degradation of some women, and the lowering to a much wider extent of the prevailing estimate of female character.

Such are some of the pleas by which the marriage bond as it exists among us, may be defended in the interests of society. They carry us but a little way towards that purity of thought and life which Jesus demanded so stringently; and in relation to the strength of human passion, and the terrible evils which follow its indulgence, they

may appear to have little power. Not by such
remote considerations, it is true, can the lawlessness of impulse be restrained, and the lives of
tempted and erring men made pure. It is one
thing to know what is right, a very different thing
to practise it.

Yet the declaration of true principles is not uncalled for and can never be useless, and to see
clearly how the welfare of society depends on the
institution of marriage, must help to encourage the
habits of personal purity and delicacy which tend
to uphold it. It may be questioned, indeed, how
far any direct attempts to deal with this subject,
whether by legislative enactment or by harangues
from the pulpit or platform, are likely to have
much success. The discerning student of human
nature must view with grave suspicion schemes
for the purification of society which consist largely
of advertisements of the devil's business. Reticence is the duty of churches and associations as
well as of individuals, and ditches are not to be
purified by gazing into them, however piously.
Men are not elevated and improved so much by
concentrating their attention on struggles with

their lower nature, as by the reinforcement of those elements of it which are healthy and spiritual. The contemplation of noble types of womanhood such as we find in Shakespeare, and the diffusion of the spirit of chivalry, such as breathes in the best modern poetry, these perhaps are the only more direct means by which a wise teacher would seek to combat the evils here in view. While stating the necessity of strenuous self-government, he would put his trust largely in means which are indirect, and would be persuaded that the soul is purified and man redeemed by work, by enthusiasm for any noble cause, by every endeavour in which he devotes himself to, or identifies himself with, truth or goodness or beauty.

THE EIGHTH COMMANDMENT.

Thou shalt not steal.

STUDYING the commandments is studying the very origin of civilisation, the A B C of human society. These simple emphatic words stand like great march-stones between the primitive world, in which men were savages, each following his own desires, and the better world in which they have begun to set up institutions and to practise self-control. We see how much the laws of God have done for man, when we try to realise what human life was before these laws were given, or had begun to be respected. What was the world like when the institution of marriage had not yet been set up, as in the seventh commandment, or before the family was regarded as a divine institution, as the fifth commandment bids us regard it, or even when there was no division of time into weeks, such as the fourth commandment sanctions? What a great step was made in the setting up of each of these great institutions, of which the commandments are as it were the memorial stones! The barbarism and chaos that lie behind them can never again come back to cover the earth, so long as men regard with reverence these venerable sentences. When men received such laws and enshrined them in general respect they ceased to be savages, they had conquered a soil in which human nature could begin to grow freely, and to put forth its manifold fruits and flowers. Any tendency to set these laws at naught is a great danger to mankind, and ought to be promptly and sternly checked, because it threatens to throw man back into the confusion and insecurity of ruder times.

What was the world like before the commandment "Thou shalt not steal" was written upon the conscience of mankind—in the days of which the poet sings:

>"The good old rule
Sufficeth them, the simple plan
That they should take who have the power,
And they should keep, who can?"

There was a time when the act of the stronger in taking from the weaker, went by a handsomer name than stealing, and was thought quite natural and fitting. If a man wanted a thing, why should he not put forth his hand and take it, if he could? Another had the good of it at present, but that could be changed, and it was rather creditable to change that state of matters in one's own favour.

How that plan worked it is easy to conceive. In such a state of society no arts could flourish greatly but the arts of war and violence. No man would work hard for a harvest which another would in all probability appropriate. People would hide their goods and pretend to be poorer than they were, so that the robber might pass them by; only the strong would dare to have more silver and gold or finer cattle, than his neighbours. All possessions being insecure, one not endowed with physical prowess nor in a position to command the services of retainers, would either have no property, or if naturally industrious, would be thrown upon the arts of stratagem and deceit, in order to conceal the fruits of his industry. There was little motive for any one to exert himself, and all improvement and progress would be at a standstill. In such a state of things the poor would suffer most; the rich man could protect himself by his servants and warriors, but the poor would have no helper, unless they placed themselves under the protection of some strong neighbour and so surrendered their independence.

But once let it come to be one of the principal doctrines of religion, that it was wrong to take away another man's possessions, and industry would begin to stir, men would seek to enlarge their belongings, and all sorts of improvements would be set on foot. Once let it be thought that when a man has honestly come by a thing, he has a sacred right to keep it, that it is his, that it is God's will that he should have it, and that he who takes away what another has acquired, breaks a divine law and is worthy of punishment, and motives at once come into play, which make men diligent, inventive, enterprising, thrifty, self-denying. The poor have hope, and each man begins to do what he can do best, in order to add to his store. The peaceful and fertilising competition of industry takes the place of rude and devastating violence. Talents are developed which formerly were hidden and unsuspected. The community is enriched in a thousand ways by the exertions men are encouraged to make, on the assurance that the fruits of these exertions will not be taken from them. And so the eighth commandment, which declares the institution of property to be a sacred institution, according to the will of God, and not to be set at naught without incurring his displeasure, marks the transition from the age of violence, when men could not improve the earth nor make the best of their own faculties, to the age of industry, in which men are stimulated to develop the resources of the world and the riches of their own nature, and human life becomes always brighter and more full of interest. And any attempt to break down the inviolableness of this institution, and to destroy the sacredness and security of property, is a grave sin against human progress. To unsettle the notion of property, and to preach that it is lawful to take away from any set of men what they have acquired, is to that extent to bring back the age of violence, to weaken the motives for industry and self-denial, to arrest the march of civilisation.

There is no doubt that the notion of property is essential to the very idea of human nature. Man without personal belongings, is a conception which it is almost impossible to realise. Early savages, perhaps, had not the notion of property; they had not attained to the distinction between body and spirit, which is essential to that notion. But it appears wherever man is civilised. The abolition of personal property would involve the disappearance of many other institutions of civilisation. Where there are no fences, there can be no home. Parents who had nothing to give their children could exercise little authority over them. Without property man would be so destitute of personal standing, so incapable of individual action, so enthralled to the public, so devoid of any interest or outlook of his own, so hopeless and dull, that he never could accomplish anything on the earth's face. If man is to be free, he must have property. And it may be asserted with little fear of contradiction, that the simple law which bids us regard our neighbour's personality as embracing not only his body, but to some extent also those things which by his labour and skill he has converted to his own uses, has been from the first an element of the human conscience, and could never by any possibility be eradicated from it. What my neighbour has made is his, is part of him; no right of man is older or more natural than this. He has created it, he has given it his own character, but for him it would not have been there. We must allow him to use it in his own way, so long as he does no harm with it; to forbid him to give it to whom he likes, would be to rob him of it at the very moment when it is most valuable to him; and if he is free to give it, the receiver also must be free to keep it. When we consider the widespread cruelty which would be involved in the abolition of this institution of property, how the hopes of the poor as well as the rich would be cut off, and the purposes of multitudes of men frustrated: how apathy would take the place of eagerness in countless lives, and willing citizenship give way to hatred of the power which had brought such a thing to pass, we must conclude that no law is more deeply seated in the interests and wishes of all men than this one, or deserves to be held more fundamental and sacred.

We are taught by Christ to consider, that the worst sin against the commandments is to teach men to break them. The worst breach of the commandment, " Thou shalt not steal," is to teach that the notion of property is wrong and ought not to be respected. It would be trifling with our subject to enumerate the different kinds of theft and fraud that men commit, and thunder against them. We might begin with speaking to children about the great difference between what belongs to them and what belongs to some one else, and say how sacred the line is, which separates the one from the other, and how little good anything can do them, how miserable any possession must make them, though they coveted it ever so earnestly, that has been taken away, stolen, from some one else. We might go on to speak of the duty of servants to be faithful with what is entrusted to them, to regard their master's property as sacred, and never enrich themselves with it. We might speak of the duty of masters to see that their servants are adequately rewarded for their labour, and deprived of none of their just rights. And we might go on to speak of rendering to all their due, of the wickedness of

hard bargains, and of all over-reaching practices
in the market and the exchange, of the strong
desire every good man must feel that those who
deal with him should get their due and not be the
worse off for the transaction. If in some walks of
life it is difficult to avoid practices which strict
honour cannot justify, there is all the more reason
for good men to turn away from them, so as both
to keep their own conscience clear, and to raise
the public standard of morality.

But the gravest sin against the eighth commandment does not, as we said, consist so much in acts
of theft, as in teaching men so ; in trying to get it
considered that property is an evil thing, and ought
not to be respected. The worst effect of any act
of theft or sharp practice lies in the impression it
produces on the mind of the doer of it and of
others. The thief loses respect for the laws of
society, because he has successfully set them at
naught, the victim loses confidence in these laws,
because they have not protected him. Such an
act is a return to the savage state, it undermines
the feelings of security, it causes all possessions

and rights to be regarded as less sacred, and to that extent unsettles the foundations of society.

But much more unsettling, much more mischievous, than any single acts of theft or fraud is the preaching of the doctrine that property is not a sacred institution, and that the owners of it, or certain classes of the owners of it, may be plundered without injustice. The doctrines which are preached on this subject, if we believed that any great number of the people seriously attended to them, might cause us great uneasiness as to the future of our country. To listen to them, we should imagine that covetousness had ceased to be a sin, or honesty a virtue. Many of the cures which are proposed for the evils of society simply amount to this, that the property of the rich should be taken from them to be given to the poor. And in support of that policy we are told that the state has a right to dispose as it likes of the property of its citizens, or to decree, should it seem good, that certain kinds of property or the whole institution of property, should come to an end; as if any state could be justified in abolishing the fundamental law on which its own existence rests. Some are far too rich, it is said; and multitudes are far too poor. The State ought to make its citizens more equal; the profits of industry must in future be more equally divided. Christianity also is appealed to, at the outset of which property was practically abolished, and the members of the Church cast their goods into a common store, for the common benefit of all.

The State can no doubt do much to increase the happiness of the poorer classes. Most of all it can insist on the improvement of education, so as to bring home to all the same mental advantages at the outset of life, and to obliterate, so far as may be possible, the differences of culture which alone really divide from each other the various classes in the state. Nor can any Christian minister fail to bow down reverently to the great Christian idea, that the goods of all are given them for the benefit of all, or to believe the good time to be coming, when that idea will be practically realised in a way which does not yet appear. But no progress can be made by disregarding the laws of nature or by slighting the laws of God written on the conscience, and that State would hinder instead of advancing the welfare of its population, which should seek to set aside the principle, that what a man has acquired or inherited, he is entitled to keep and to use according to his own judgment, as long as he does not use it in a way that is mischievous to others. Robbery is not any more respectable when it is committed by a democracy than when it is the act of a king or baron, and it must tend even more, when it is the act of a people, to unsettle confidence and check industry. Nor can that good time which Christianity promises to us,—the time when again it shall be true that no man says that the things which he possesses are his own, but they have all things common,—ever be advanced by spoliation. It must come not by taking, but by giving: not by forbidding individuals to hold property, but by getting it to be believed more warmly and more generally (and this is already coming), that the way to get most happiness out of it, is to spread the blessing that is in it over as many as possible. But if property is to be used in this way, it must be property, it must be secure.

In the meantime let us strive to be content, and

not to covet that which is not ours. To me perhaps God has given little, to others he has given more; but what I have I can use honestly, cheerfully, with dignity, with generosity; shaping my desires to be well within my means, and owing no man anything but love.

THE NINTH COMMANDMENT.

Thou shalt not bear false witness against thy neighbour.

When we arrive at this commandment and look it in the face, our first feeling is one of surprise. The sin it denounces is a rare one. When only ten commandments were being given, how was it that the sin of perjury got one to itself? Was the bearing of false witness a common offence among the people to whom the commandments were addressed, so that it required such particular notice? And is that offence so important that it should be expressly prohibited, and should receive a place in the same category with murder and adultery and theft?

As to the first question, whether the sin of perjury was common among the Jews, the Old Testament affords some ground for thinking that it was. There are about half-a-dozen proverbs describing the character of the false witness, and the thief and the false witness seem to have frequently worked in partnership. We know how easily false witnesses were found to testify against Naboth in the interests of a royal intrigue; and they are also spoken of in the New Testament, in connection with the trial of our Lord and with that of Stephen. And in some of the Psalms we meet with complaints of this kind of wickedness; as where it is said, "False witnesses are risen up against me, and such as breathe out cruelty."

When we try to conceive of a state of things in which such an offence was not uncommon, we see at once—should we not have thought of this before—what a grave offence it is, what a fatal weapon it supplies to the hands of unscrupulous men, what a serious danger it is to society. Society can have no stability if the administration of justice is not pure. The object of society, a great philosopher has said, is to support the twelve judges. If the thief and the false witness hunt in couples and supply the judges with false information, if our enemy meets us at the source of justice with a story he has made up for our destruction, and has got others to swear to, then it is plain that the object of society is not secured. It has failed to protect us, and we are led to wish ourselves back in a simpler state of society, where we could carve out justice with our own right hand. It was a great improvement in human affairs when men gave up being judge and officer in their own causes, and appointed magistrates, who should have power to remedy injustice and settle disputes. But if the ear of the magistrate is filled with falsehood, then the rule of violence is not at an end; murder and theft still flourish, only in a more insidious form, and are accomplished through the forms of law. The object of civil institutions is not attained.

Thus we see that civilisation cannot be upheld without the practice of truth-speaking on the part of those who are to dwell together. Lying is as fatal to civil order as murder and theft. "Speak every man truth to his neighbour," says the apostle, "because ye are members one of another." His words go to the root of the matter. We cannot be members one of another, we cannot live together in an organised society or carry on any common enterprise, except on the condition that we speak the truth when called on to do so. The State has a right to know the truth, and to call on the citizens to state what they have seen and heard, in any matter affecting the public. The State cannot possibly permit false witness in its courts of justice, and must always prosecute perjury, where there is reason to think it has taken place. Should it be thought that perjury could be committed with impunity, no one would be safe; the alliance between the thief and the false witness would flourish afresh, and private hatred would seek its gratification by conspiracy carried through the courts of justice with the aid of false swearing. The State must check perjury wherever it appears, and must make it felt and understood, that the offence is one which cannot be pardoned.

In this commandment, accordingly, we see a third clause of the great charter of freedom and toleration, of which we saw the earlier provisions in the sixth and eighth commandments. In these laws the natural man finds one weapon after another struck from his hands, by which he might be inclined to ease himself of his adversaries. Those whom you dislike, he is told, are not to be put away by murder, they are not to be robbed, they are not to be pursued with slanders. You must leave them in the enjoyment of life, of property, of reputation, you must not interfere with the position which it has pleased God to give them. Whatever you dislike about them, their policy, or their superior wealth, or their reputation overshadowing your own, you must not stretch forth your hands against them in any of these ways; they must leave you your place, your possessions, your good report, and you must leave them theirs. You must either tolerate them to this extent, and leave them undisturbed, to enjoy their goods and exercise their abilities, or lose the favour of Heaven. God forbids you to invade them in any of these ways.

It is a very small modicum of truthfulness that this commandment asks for. Regarded literally, it asks no more than that when we are called to speak publicly of a matter affecting our neighbour, we should give true evidence; and that we should bring forward no false charge against him. It may not happen to us during our whole lifetime to be called upon for evidence. It is certainly a small thing to require, that we should make no public assault upon our neighbour, by saying what is untrue about him.

The commandment does not set up an ideal of truthfulness. None of the commandments sets up an ideal. They do not tell us the highest to aim at for personal virtue, they tell us the lowest, the minimum of self-restraint which men must exercise, if they are to live together in a society. The commandments are not a standard of virtue: a poor standard these bald prohibitions would be: they are a constitution, they prescribe the bases of a community. They are not ethical precepts, they are laws, and are addressed not to our motives, but to our acts.

At the same time a law which requires us to speak truth on certain occasions, must certainly be found in practice to involve the exercise of truthful habits generally. The people which is not truthful in the market and the street, will not be truthful in the court of justice either. If it is not our habit to speak the truth, if we have a feeble sense of the importance of truth, and are given to say what suits us, or to exaggerate what has come under our notice, then we shall be ill-prepared to speak truth on those outstanding occasions, when our word is specially asked for. The law-courts of this and other countries proceed on the assumption that people are not to be trusted to speak the truth in court without swearing that they will do so. Left to themselves, it is assumed, without the stimulant of an oath, they are liable to deviate from the truth; the oath will keep them straight. But a man's mind will work in its ordinary groove even though he goes through that ceremony; the oath will furnish him with no new faculties to see things plain, if he is in the habit of seeing them distorted. And the law would teach a higher lesson to the country, if it proceeded on the assumption that a man's ordinary statement is as sacred as an oath can make it, and that even the untruth which is spoken without any oath, is in the highest degree wrong, and deserving of punishment.

Habitual truth-speaking is thus indirectly commanded by the ninth commandment, because those who do not speak truth habitually, cannot be depended on to speak truth when their evidence is called for publicly. We can have no right at any time, or in any company, to injure a fellow-creature by our manner of speaking of him. The character of others is a part of their goods of which we can never be entitled to deprive them, and with which we must always deal carefully and justly. They have a right to demand of us, that whenever we speak of them we should at least speak truthfully. We undoubtedly break this commandment whenever we allow ourselves, for whatever reason, to misrepresent their acts, or to impute to them unworthy motives, by which we cannot know that they are guided, or to repeat disagreeable stories about them, which we cannot know to be true. It is not only in the court of justice that we are forbidden to wrong them by false evidence. In the larger court of general opinion, which holds its sittings wherever men converse, and where the character of men and actions is perpetually being weighed, there also we are forbidden to speak inaccurately, or rashly, or with prejudice. There also we are bound to make our words correspond as nearly as we can to the facts we speak of. There also it is incumbent on us to divest ourselves of exaggeration and confusion, and to say not what we wish to be the case, nor what we merely fancy, nor what we have heard but have taken no trouble to verify. We must say what we see to be the fact, so far as our insight extends, and where it fails, we must be silent, lest we should bear false witness against our neighbour.

For a striking example of the breach of this commandment as it thus applies to common life, we have only to look at the manner in which political controversy is in too many quarters conducted. The ordinary method of many politicians consists simply in blackening the character of their opponents. The public are invited to regard the leaders of one of the great parties, as monsters who can never be guided by reasonable or patriotic motives, to attach to their utterances the worst possible meaning, and to see in their policy nothing but a tissue of personal ambition, jealousy and cunning. It will be well if God grant us not to give ear to such bearing of false witness against public men, as is plentifully practised among us.

There is something higher surely to be seen in politics than the play of mean personalities; there are principles at work, and he only can form a true judgment of the leaders of the State, who is candid enough and calm enough to understand and do justice to the principles which they maintain. In these high matters, as well as in the talk about persons which forms so large a part of the world's conversation, the truth is not to be attained, and injustice is not to be avoided, without a certain effort. The charity which rejoices not in iniquity but rejoices in the truth, is an intellectual virtue, and comes from that earnestness of mind which cannot rest in shallow and one-sided judgments, but presses to attain a clear and rational understanding of men and things. If we are not to injure others by our words about them, we must endeavour, in the words of a great philosopher, "not to hate them, nor to fear them, nor to ridicule them, but to understand them." Truth is always just, and no one can ask more than that what is said of him be true. If we seek earnestly to understand others, we shall be saved from saying anything about them that we would not dare to say if they were present.

There is a higher reason for truthfulness than this commandment suggests to us. The commandment only warns us against such departures from the truth as may injure other people, but a more absolute warning sounds in the heart of the good man, against all untruthfulness, whether it be injurious to others or no, because whatever it may be to others, it must be fatal to himself. This is one of the results of that immeasurable elevation of the sacredness and dignity of the individual soul, which Christianity produced. There are those, and every Christian should be of them, to whom it is not possible to be consciously false on any subject, whom nothing would induce to take such shame upon them. They cannot understand how men should lie for gain or from conceit; such an act appears to them like casting in the mire a priceless jewel, to secure a handful of chaff instead. How, such a one feels inclined to ask, can men humiliate themselves, give up their soul, cast to the winds all that makes them men, to reap a slight and perishing advantage, or to gratify a transient feeling?

Such truthfulness is the salt of society, the salvation of the state; it is the quality which more than any other makes men the citizens of a better world, and gives them power to make this world better. Perhaps God has not cast us all in such a noble mould, nor given to us such spirits like diamonds, translucent and incapable of stain. But the fact that we are able to admire such virtue, and to be persuaded of it, and by faith embrace it, even if from afar, shows that we also are made for it. To practice it even imperfectly, in our teaching, in our thinking, in our acts, and in our conversation, is the best we can do for our fellow-creatures, by far the best for ourselves.

THE TENTH COMMANDMENT.

Thou shalt not covet.

This commandment, we at once observe, is different from the rest. All the others speak of our actions, and enjoin upon us to do certain things, and leave certain things undone. The laws with which we have been dealing require us to keep our hands off our neighbour's person and property, and not to assail him unjustly with our tongue. They make our neighbour sacred in our eyes, they fence in the various interests of each member of the community with religious barriers which we dare not overstep, and so secure to him his liberty and independence, the fruits of his industry, his domestic happiness, his reputation. By thus forbidding all encroachment on his rights they lay the foundations of the social structure, and guarantee the peace and order of the community.

But the natural man will not keep such laws. Men will not keep them unless in some way trained and prepared to do so, because these laws are contrary to the earliest impulses men have. The law says, Thou shalt not do this and that; but these are just the things which passion when strongly excited prompts men to do; the law bids us tolerate those whom we dislike, but our impulses do not incline us to toleration, and claim to be gratified as quickly as possible. And the behest of an invisible law-giver will be a feeble check on us, the ideal barriers which fence in our neighbour and his goods and interests, will be a frail defence, if our impulses have not been trained in some way to submission, and if we are still such untamed creatures of impulse as the beasts of the forests are, or some tribes of uncivilised men. Desire is blind; it knows no scruple in the choice of its instruments; it recks not of the grief and ruin it may cause in the pursuit of its objects. If it is not curbed and governed, it will stick at no crime; human rights will not arrest its course, divine prohibitions will not restrain it. As the Apostle says, "there is another law in our members, which is not subject to the law of God." If therefore society is to exist, if men are to live together, enjoying each other's help and leaving each other unmolested, it is not enough that acts of violence should be forbidden and should be punished by the state; for desires when they are allowed to grow to their full height in man's breast, set at naught all prohibitions and disregard all consequences. Men must not only receive the law, they must also prepare themselves to keep it. To be good citizens of a state, men must learn to keep their desires in check; they must keep down the impulses, which if indulged would lead to crime, they must set to work within themselves, and accustom themselves not to desire what they cannot righteously obtain. And so the Decalogue closes with a commandment which requires self-discipline, and tells us not to covet anything that is our neighbour's. In the tenth commandment it passes from national to personal religion, and points forward to New Testament times.

We often hear it stated as an excuse for some one who has done wrong, that his impulses were so strong, so overmastering, as to leave him no choice in his actions. We may observe in many quarters an inclination to think, that when people desire any thing very much, they ought to get it, that when the desire for a thing reaches a certain pitch of vehemence, it constitutes a claim to the possession of it. Every criminal will account to you in this way for the commission of his crime. He ordered goods he could not pay for, because he could not really do without them. He took what was another's, because such a powerful desire for it came over him. Or he committed some other crime, because his impulses were such that he thought it necessary to obey them. So the desire which led to the transgression is regarded by the transgressor, and often by others too, as an excuse for it. This logic of the feelings is a process with which we are all familiar. Surely, we think, we must be meant to have what we desire so strongly. Surely it cannot be intended that our heart should waste its energies in fruitless longings. A pleasure or a possession that would suit us so well, which no one can use so well as we could, which indeed cannot fulfil its true destiny till it is ours, and with which our desires and tendencies already so

strongly connect us, must we not have it, is it not
ours by right, are not the barriers which keep us
from it mere man-made conventions, which should
yield to the truth of the matter, so plainly written
upon our minds? So speaks the pathos of the
heart, the eloquence of desire: so does desire persuade a man that theft is right, that adultery is
natural and fit, that murder is not so wrong as it
is generally held to be.

And here comes this commandment, the hardest
surely of them all, and tells us that such desires,
far from being any excuse for lawless acts, are
themselves wrong and wicked, and ought not to
be listened to for a moment, but plucked up by the
roots from the heart in which they have appeared.
To say that a man did such and such a crime
because his feelings were so strong, because, poor
man, he had so vehement a wish for a thing that
was otherwise beyond his reach, may explain to
some extent the history of his crime, but does not
make it any better. Coveting does not excuse
theft, or any other sin: it is itself a sin, which the
man should not have committed. The desire
should not have been indulged. When you desire

something very strongly, that you cannot get in a righteous way, it is true that you are in a difficulty, it is true that you suffer and have torment; but the right way out of such a difficulty is not to follow the desire, but to put it down, to refuse to yield to it, to declare to yourself that the thing you desire is a thing you simply are not to get, a thing that is out of the question.

And thus the heart is deposed from the position which belongs to it in infancy, and which, though human life is no longer in its infancy, some would still ascribe to it, of being the rule of our conduct, the dictator of our acts. It is not man's heart, not his desires, that are to tell him how to act; if that were the case there could be no such thing as settled and peaceful society. The state of nature, to which many are inclined to look back as the best and happiest state man was ever in, that state, if there was ever such a state, in which men were not controlled by laws, and in which they did not need to deny themselves, but could follow without hesitation the instincts of their hearts,—it could not be a good state to live in, and it is not God's will that we should return to it. In no age of the world in which desire was unrestricted, could there be any peace or order. It is only through the strait gate of self-control, that man could enter in any age into social happiness. In an age which regarded the desires as naturally entitled to be satisfied, the pleasure derived from one's own licensed selfishness would be far outweighed by the inconvenience suffered from the licensed selfishness of others. Each man would be against his neighbour, all consideration of others would be put aside, all regard for their tastes and feelings, nay, for their life and property; all constraints would be spurned, all laws set at nought. If the tenth commandment be not kept, all the rest will prove but idle wind; selfishness once set up as ruler, will find plausible excuses for putting them all aside. The tenth commandment was given to us that it might be possible for us to keep the others. We are bidden to begin to keep the law of God deep in our hearts, and to set to work there to prune down the desires which, if allowed to grow, would carry us into lawlessness. We are to keep our eyes from wandering, to teach ourselves contentment, and to regard all that is our neighbour's as sacred, not only against lawless acts, but also against wandering imaginations and desires.

If we are forbidden to covet that which is not ours, it is plain that we must turn to that which is our own, and either be content with it, or if we are not content with it, seek to increase and improve it by our own industry. Men will never cease to desire what they have not yet attained, it would be vain to bid them never desire more than they have, and it would also be mischievous, for the extinction of desire is the extinction of life itself, the cessation of all effort, the death of progress. But though I am forbidden to look over my neighbour's fence, and covet what I see about his homestead, I am not forbidden to carry out all the improvements I can on my own farm. That is what the tenth commandment implies that I must do, it bids me seek the fulfilment of my desires, not in what may come to me from without, but in what I can do for myself. A man is not to covet his neighbour's wife. He must pour into his own marriage all the grace and affection he can, until he feels, as all those who are truly married

feel, that the primeval romance of prince and
princess united after many sorrows in an indissoluble bond, is realised in their own case, and that
there never was a sweeter union than their own.
He is not to set his affection on his neighbour's
cattle; then, to increase his store, he must improve
his own, and make the best of them. Does he
want more land? He is not to covet that which
is not his, nor to lay hands upon it by open
violence or by political agitation. He must desire
nothing that he cannot obtain legitimately, but he
can use the land he has so well, that more will be
entrusted to him. Does he want to be richer, to
have more wages and an easier life? He must
not seek to gain those ends by denouncing the
rich or by voting for their spoliation, but by using
the vigour and the skill God has given him, to the
best advantage. He must not hearken to those
who bid him expect salvation to come to him from
without, by that being added to him which at present belongs to others, but must consider that his
help must be wrought out by himself, by his own
industry and self-denial.

This is the plan that men must follow if they

are to live together, peacefully and happily, and to have a good conscience towards each other and towards God. The old plans of enriching ourselves and setting ourselves on high in comparison with others, we must consider that we have forever left behind us, in that earlier and ruder world, from which the laws of God were given to set us free. Robbery, murder, adultery, and slander,—they are all relics of the barbarism from which we boast that we have escaped. They belong to an earlier state of things; in the settled order which God and man together have set up, and which, with God's help, we are determined to maintain, they can have no place; when they do occur among us, we must mark emphatically that they are not allowed. But gone with them too, if they are gone, must be the selfish and unregulated impulses which gave birth to them: the man of the new order is not a creature of impulse, but one to whose mind the rights and liberties of others are ever present, and who regulates his conduct not by his impulses but by fixed rules and principles. Gone too must the old notion be, that the prosperity of one man is an insult or a challenge to his neighbours, and calls them to enrich themselves by plundering him, or to exalt themselves by pulling him down. Instead of the narrow and selfish views belonging to the early state of mankind, we are called to cherish a more generous and at the same time a more practical view, namely, that the way to advance ourselves is to work diligently with our own resources, that others must be left free to do all they can with theirs, and that when each is left free to do his utmost with his own gifts in his own sphere, society is most advantaged, men are happiest, and the intentions of the great and All-Wise Founder of our state most fully realised.

Notes on some Books of Special Interest

PUBLISHED BY

ALEXANDER GARDNER,

PAISLEY AND LONDON.

AT ALL LIBRARIES.

JAMES HEPBURN, *Free Church Minister*.
By SOPHIE F. F. VEITCH, Author of "Angus Graeme, Gamekeeper," etc. 2 vols., Crown 8vo., 21s.

"A strong story of real life and cannot fail to give Miss Veitch a prominent position among modern novelists. . . . The whole story is exceedingly powerful."– *Saturday Review.*

"The work of fiction which heads the list may fairly be described as **a singularly powerful and fascinating novel.** Description by comparison is frequently convenient, though occasionally misleading; but we do not think we shall convey a wrong impression if we say that 'James Hepburn' bears a strong resemblance to some of the most vigorous and characteristic of Mrs. Oliphant's realistic Scottish stories. . . . James Hepburn is one of the most truly heroic characters in recent fiction, with a certain largeness and grandeur in his heroism which are wonderfully impressive, and yet with a homeliness which never permits him to slip for a moment outside the range of our imaginative belief. In creating an ideal character of unmistakable flesh and blood, Miss Veitch has achieved an unequivocal success, and one or two of the pivot situations in the book are conceived and presented with such dramatic power and sympathetic insight, that in virtue of them alone 'James Hepburn' takes place among the most remarkable and admirable of recent novels. . . . There are chapters in 'James Hepburn' of which we feel convinced that the author of *Scenes of Clerical Life* would not have been ashamed. . . . Such a novel is not only a book to admire, but one for which to be grateful."—*The Spectator.*

"'James Hepburn' is a novel in two volumes, which is quite startling in the freshness and beauty of its conception. . . . This book deserves careful reading; there is much more in it than the mere interest of a clever story, and only good can result from its influence."— *Literary World.*

"The author of 'Angus Graeme, Gamekeeper,' has produced another Scottish novel of remarkable power. 'James Hepburn, Free Church Minister,' is at once a striking character study, a skilful picture of the social life of a country town and district, and a powerful sensational story. It is in the first of these aspects that it displays most original vigour. . . . It must be admitted to be one of the strongest productions of the fictional art that have recently appeared."— *Scotsman.*

"There can be no question that 'James Hepburn' is the most notable Scottish story that will be issued in the jubilee year."—*The Christian Leader.*

"And of this tendency towards pure character-painting and everyday incident Miss Sophie Veitch promises to be the best exponent. In the two volumes which contain the story of episodes in the life of James Hepburn, each character is carefully studied and presented as a finished masterpiece. . . . The book is a drama palpitating with intense and real life, whose author should have a grand professional future."—*Whitehall Review.*

"The book deserves the highest praise. Hepburn's relations with Lady Ellinor—his pure and noble love for her—are fitly crowned by his splendid self-sacrifice. . . . The descriptive part of this fine and often brilliant novel is admirably done."—*London Figaro.*

"No one who begins this story will pause till he has seen the hero through his troubles, and we are sure no one who has done so will think he has spent his time badly."—*The British Weekly.*

James Hepburn is a story of very unusual power, promise, and desert. . . . The story of Lady Elinor is exceedingly pathetic; and all her moods, as she gradually progresses along a path of peril, are described with a hand at once sure and delicate.—*Academy.*

Seldom do we meet with a novel by a comparatively unknown author which can afford such unalloyed pleasure. . . . It is not every writer who can, like Mrs. Oliphant, throw a glamour over the sordid details of *bourgeois* life. Amongst the few who can do so Miss Veitch may now claim to rank; her novel is a remarkable one, and if it does not attain to considerable popularity the fault will not be with the author. . . . There is intense pathos in the loyal struggle of the beautiful young wife who believes herself to be unsympathised with. . . . We had marked more than one passage for quotation, but space warns us that the pleasure must be forgone. We must, however, draw special attention to Lady Ellinor's withering summary of Radicalism (vol. ii. p. 242). The novel is one of the very few that follows Mr. Weller's recipe, and makes us "wish that there was more of it."—*Pictorial World.*

"A SUCCESSFUL SCOTCH NOVEL.—It is long since a Scottish novel met with such a demand or created such a genuine sensation as has attended the publication of 'James Hepburn, Free Church Minister,' which was issued a few weeks ago by Mr. Gardner, of Paisley, and which we noticed in the week of its publication. We hear that already Mr. Mudie has ordered four separate supplies, the latest being for a large number of copies, so great is the demand for the story on the part of the subscribers to his library. Miss Sophie Veitch, the authoress, had already made her mark by her fine novel of 'Angus Graeme, Gamekeeper.'"—*Daily Mail.*

"'James Hepburn,' by Miss Veitch, is a *clever and strong* novel. . . . Its power and literary skill are undeniable."—*World.*

"Novel-readers who may think there is not much promise of entertainment in the title which Sophie F. Veitch has chosen for her new story, will commit the common blunder of forming an erroneous judgment from superficial appearances. A more interesting or vigorously-written tale we have not met with for some time back."—*The Scottish Leader.*

"A cleverly written story here includes both interesting incident and well-drawn character."—*The Queen.*

SUPPLEMENT TO JAMIESON'S SCOTTISH DICTIONARY. By DAVID DONALDSON. Now Ready, Price 25s.; Large Paper, 42s.

"The work, taken as a whole, entitles Mr. Donaldson to the gratitude of all interested in the study of philology, for having performed so thoroughly and so well a difficult and laborious task."—*Scotsman.*

"The soundness of the judgment which he has applied to this portion of his herculean task is only equalled by the fulness of his knowledge of those works which cover the whole period of Scottish history, during which the vernacular was written and spoken by all classes of society. A very large number of the words in the Supplement are recorded by Mr. Donaldson for the first time, at least as Scottish words, and of many of them the explanation will be found nowhere else. . . Of Mr. Donaldson's work, it may safely be said that it is the most complete and scholarly endeavour that has thus far been made to accomplish a very difficult task."—*Mail.*

"On every page we find evidence that Mr. Donaldson has mastered all the works that cover the entire period of Scottish history during which the vernacular was written and spoken by all classes of society. He has, furthermore, utilised an extensive personal knowledge derived from the living speech of the people; and alike in the definitions and illustrations he displays unfailing soundness of judgment, shown sometimes as much in what he has omitted as in that which is given. An excellent memoir of Dr. Jamieson, admirable both for the fullness of its information and the generous warmth of its spirit, adds to the value of a work without which, we may safely affirm, no Scottish library can henceforth be regarded as complete."—*Leader.*

IDYLL OF THE CAPTIVE KING; and

Other Pieces. With Etchings. By JAMES SHARP. Crown 8vo, cloth, 6s.

"The author gives undoubted evidence of his right to be heard, and our perusal of this volume enables us to commend his wide reading and knowledge of the world, both in its physical and ethical aspects. It is needless to add that Mr. Gardner has done his part admirably."—*The Kelso Chronicle.*

"Whether Mr. Sharp's poetry be regarded in the abstract, or as the product of the hours of leisure of a man of business, much of it is commendable, and much is genuine and sound in feeling."—*The Scottish News.*

Mr. James Sharp does not miss the occasion in his volume of poems, *The Captive King* (Alexander Gardner). His Jubilee Ode, like those of better-known bards, scarcely represents his poetic powers, as the following couplet may show:—

Much as we love the Prince of Wales, the Princess fair, serene,
We want no other sovereign! We want no other Queen!

"Tullibardine's Bride," though a little diffuse, is a readable narrative poem based on a Perthshire legend. In other lyrical pieces Mr. Sharp sustains a patriotic vein with fervour.—*Saturday Review.*

Mr. Sharp's lyrics and shorter pieces, are always pleasing in sentiment, and are often sweet in expression.—*Scotsman.*

The book of poems which we introduce to our readers to-day has, we think, amply justified its issue in the beautiful form in which it is presented to the public. . . . This delightful book will do something to modify that conception, and to show that mercantile pursuits and the exalted, if traditionally prosaic, dignity of Bailieship are not incompatible with a successful cultivation of the Muses. In depicting one of the most tragic chapters in our national annals, Mr. Sharp has attained charming results in his use of those heroic measures which the genius of Scott and of Edmonstone Aytoun has made classic, and through which these masters have made the dim shadows that erewhile flitted across the stage of Scottish history to stand forth as living men. . . . We have directed the attention of our readers to these poems because of their intrinsic merits.—*Strathearn Herald.*

If it be the poet's task to feel pleasure in life and discern beauty in nature, to praise virtue and rejoice in love, and make his readers do the same, then Mr. Sharp has succeeded admirably in effecting his purpose.—*Dundee Advertiser.*

Mr. Sharp is seen at his best in his shorter poems. In these, as a rule, healthy sentiment is expressed in unpretentious verse.—*Academy.*

SECOND AND ENLARGED EDITION.

LAW LYRICS. Fcap. 8vo, 3s. 6d.

"The anonymous author of the 'Lyrics'—is he not to be met with among the sheriffs?—plays his tunes for session and vacation on the 'goose-quill' of the law,' and he manages to produce from that ancient instrument a considerable variety of expression. . . . His pronounced national tastes are admirably shown in 'Oatmeal,' etc.; in lyrics like 'Stornoway Bay,' there is the true lyrical gush; while in such poems as 'A Still Lake,' there is revealed an exquisite power of word-painting. . ."—*Scotsman.*

"For neatness and aptness of expression, it is equal to anything we have seen."—*Scots Law Review.*

"A very agreeable little book for an idle hour. The author shows himself equally at home in the serious as in the comic."—*Graphic.*

"They are exceedingly clever, and brimming over with fun and humour. The author has earned a right to be called the Laureate of the Law, for certain it is that he invests the most prosaic of all professions with quite a halo of poetical interest."—*Nonconformist.*

"Unkempt enthusiasm and rollicking good humour are the chief features of this little volume."—*Academy.*

"A charming little book. We should seek the author on the bench, not at the bar."—*Glasgow Daily Mail.*

"Will please not only those 'gentlemen of the long robe' to whom the tiny volume is dedicated, but a far larger circle. It is a delightful book of verses daintily got up."—*Glasgow Herald.*

"These lyrics will bear comparison with the best work that has been done in this particular line Will rival some of the best of Outram's lyrics in common sense and humour."—*Scottish News.*

"The lyrics are written for the most part with sprightliness and ease. The more serious and imaginative pieces disclose a rich vein of poetic fancy. There are many who will procure the second edition from a recollection of the pleasure which the first gave them."—*Journal of Jurisprudence.*

"Will bear comparison with Outram's, Neave's, and Aytoun's. Faultless in rhythm, and remarkable for rhyme."—*Evening News.*

"The picture seems to us exquisite. Altogether, the work proves the writer to be a true poet."—*Stirling Advertiser.*

"The verses are inspirited and inspiring, expressive of the feelings of many in these golden days of summer. To the second edition the author has added some sixty pages brimful of the delightful verses which are found so attractive in the first edition."—*Weekly Citizen.*

"One of the two strongest and purest writers in the Scottish vernacular that have been added to the choir of Northern minstrels during the present century."—*Christian Leader.*

"The admirable *Law Lyrics* . . . bright with strokes of pawky humour, and abounding in verses each of which contains a picture, the volume is one which will become a lasting favourite with its readers."—*The Bailie.*

"Strongly incentive to hearty honest laughter which makes the heart grow brighter, while to staid and grave and reverend seigniors the sweet lark-song-like verses relating to nature, no less form subjects for reflection."—*Ayrshire Weekly News.*

"The little volume is interesting from the first page to the last."—*Inverness Courier.*

"Some of the verses exhibit a power of picturesque description which it would be difficult to match, except out of the masters of song. Reveal in attractive style the patriotism which animates the poet, and establishes a claim additional to that of his undoubted genius, to a large and appreciative Scotch audience."—*Greenock Telegraph.*

"Such pieces as 'Scotch Porridge, etc.' are amongst the most felicitous examples of Scotch poetry we have seen in recent years."—*Brechin Advertiser.*

"Strong common sense pervades the whole, and the views of the author are expressed with a directness, force, clearness, and simplicity, which leaves nothing to be desired."—*North British Advertiser.*

"Of a highly captivating nature, the author being possessed of a keen sense of the humourous."—*Stirling Observer.*

"Equal to anything of their kind known to us after Burns. A very genial and enjoyable volume."—*Aberdeen Gazette.*

"He expresses himself with a felicity and pawky humour that equal Lord Neaves and Outram at their best, and in several poems the natural grace and pith of expression remind one more of Burns than any other writer. This may seem pitching it very high, but in our opinion, the poems will bear out the assertion. We recommend it to all in the profession of its author, and to everyone who can appreciate true humour and good poetry."—*The People's Friend.*

"Many of the lyrics which celebrate the charms of rural life and scenery are extremely fine, displaying as they do rare observing powers, a rich fancy, and flowing tasteful language."—*Dumfries Standard.*

"He is a follower of Robert Burns and finds in the Court, and in the Temple, an inspiration which the great Scotch poet found in the fields of Ayrshire."—*Pall Mall Gazette.*

"He possesses the power of writing simple flowing verse in an eminent degree."—*Literary World.*

THE SURVIVAL OF THE FITTEST AND THE SALVATION OF THE FEW. A Criticism of *Natural Law in the Spiritual World.* By Rev. A. WILSON. Crown 8vo, cloth, 2s. 6d. Post free.

"In a former number of this *Review* we drew attention to two or three of the main fallacies of Professor Drummond's shallow but attractive book. We are glad to see that Mr. Alexander Wilson has, with a scientific knowledge equal to Professor Drummond's, and with a logical faculty far superior, subjected it to a far more systematic and exhaustive analysis. Those who were interested in the dazzling pages of *Natural Law in the Spiritual World,* but not blinded by their glitter, will welcome this justification of their doubts in the solid form of facts and arguments, and those who were fascinated by the Professor's brilliant rhetoric and imagery will have a rather painful awakening. They will see the idol shattered which they had to fall down and worship as a condition of attaining to an intellectual standpoint from which they might see all known facts in their harmony and continuity. It is, no doubt, very fascinating to be able to harmonize and to systematize ; but suppose your theory of law, identical in the natural and in the spiritual worlds, results in the necessity of assuming that man is nothing more than a part of material nature until he is "converted," and of believing that the survival of the fittest means the salvation of the few (according to the analogy of the seeds of an orchid, of about one person in a generation), would a God who has made men so be the object of religious feeling, or this spiritual world, with its rare and lonely tenants, be worth arguing for? It is probable that few readers of this new "analogy" drew such inferences, but were merely interested in Professor Drummond's spiritual and scientific gymnastics; but for the thoughtful few who may have been disturbed by them it is well that he has been answered by one so capable, both from a Christian and scientific point of view, as Mr. Wilson."—*Saturday Review.*

"It is this fallacy, the presumption that the laws of matter are continuous through the spiritual universe, that Mr. Wilson finds himself first called on to meet; and he does so by contending that the principle of continuity applies only if the spiritual universe be itself material, and not necessarily even them, inasmuch as there are in the material universe imponderable bodies to which the law of gravitation, for example, does not extend. . . . Mr. Wilson has written a very able, acute, and temperate criticism, in a thoroughly religious spirit, with perfect courtesy to his opponent; and we should be glad to think that his work would be widely read."—*Scotsman.*

". . . The critique is interesting, clever, earnest, and, we may add, respectful to Professor Drummond. . . . Here, we think, Mr. Wilson occupies a very strong—indeed, an invulnerable position. This is not, however, so much the critic's own position as that of other writers, but, he appears to us, in great measure, to recognise and accept it. His own words farther on are: 'The identification of the natural and spiritual laws, if taken absolutely, would lead to the confounding together of mind and body, God and Nature.' . . . We are much interested in the author's criticism of the Professor's arguments touching the subject which gives the book its title. It forms an earnest and powerful chapter. . . . ."—*Literary World.*

"An answer to Professor Drummond, a work of some importance has just made its appearance. It is certain that Mr. Wilson's able examination of 'Natural Law in the Spiritual World' will attract a good deal of attention and controversy."—*London Figaro.*

"Mr. Wilson, with great vigour and intrepidity, criticises the Professor's conclusions. . . . The great question raised by Professor Drummond's work is that of the relation of the natural law of the survival of the fittest to the doctrine of election. His critic combats this conclusion with much acuteness and ability."—*Glasgow Herald.*

WITH PORTRAIT AND NUMEROUS ILLUSTRATIONS.

DAVID KENNEDY, The Scottish Singer:
Reminiscences of his Life and Work. By MARJORY KENNEDY. And *SINGING ROUND THE WORLD: A Narrative of his Colonial and Indian Tours.* By DAVID KENNEDY, Junr. Demy 8vo, 480 pages, cloth extra, 7s. 6d. Post free.

"These unique musical tours were from time to time described by the chief musician's son David in different books having reference to the Colonies, to India, and to the Cape. They have now found a graceful and appropriate preliminary chapter in the form of a memoir of David Kennedy himself. . . . The memoir has been prepared by Miss Marjory Kennedy with much taste and judgment, and will be read with interest, not only for the sake of her father's characteristic letters and stories of early life, but as recalling in various other ways pleasant memories associated with a family of rare gifts and graces."—*Glasgow Herald.*

LIFE IN SHETLAND. By JOHN RUSSELL.
Crown 8vo, Cloth, 3s. 6d.   Post free.

"Contains a great quantity of very interesting information about Shetland and its people. By a happy instinct, Mr. Russell has been led to write about those things which he knows thoroughly—namely, his own doings and experiences. . . . There follows the story of the strange minister at the 'second diet' of a Presbytery meeting who wanted to propose a toast, but was informed by the horrified moderator that 'God's people in that part of the country were not in the habit of drinking toasts.' The rebuked stranger quietly rejoined that he 'had never before seen God's people drink so much toddy.' Much, both edifying and entertaining, might be quoted from this unique volume, but enough may have been said to gain for it the public attention it deserves."—*Scotsman.*

"We owe much to men like Mr. Russell, who, without any pretence, note down what comes under their observation of an interesting nature regarding curious customs, habits of life, and folk-lore, among the people with whom they come into contact. . : . He is never entirely dull, and we prefer such volumes which bring us into actual contact with a poor but unsophisticated people to many pretentious stories. We follow the minister as he goes out and in among the people, suffering hardship, visiting, catechising, getting up a stock of fifty sermons, relating odd anecdotes, and noting down peculiarities. We recommend this book to all who are interested in the subject. It makes luminous to us the obscure lives and labours of an interesting people."—*Pen and Pencil.*

"An interesting and thoroughly realistic picture of life in Shetland is presented to us in this volume by Mr. Russell, whose sojourn in those Northern islands gave him good opportunity of observing the place and the people. . . . Good stories, and brief observations and remarks on the geology, natural history, and antiquities of the islands, and the peculiar manners and customs of the people, ever and anon crop out in the narrative. . . . It contains, however, a faithfully accurate and very reliable description of *Ultima Thule.* And as the reader closes the volume he will find that he has made acquaintance at once with a singular country, and a pleasant guide to its chief points of interest."—*Aberdeen Free Press.*

"A bright and entertaining volume, and a valuable volume withal, anent Shetland and the Shetlanders. . . . I know no book on Shetland equal to this of Mr. Russell's. Its style is pointed and racy; the author talks about what he knows and what he knows intimately. To put the matter in a word, there isn't a dull page in 'Three Years in Shetland,' from the title to the sentence at the close in which Mr. Russell expresses the wish that 'all good things may attend' the islanders among whom he spent three delightful years."—*Bailie.*

"A very readable book about a very interesting people. . . . A minister, of course, enjoys altogether exceptional opportunities, and Mr. Russell seems to have made good use of them. He writes frankly about things as he found them, which he is perhaps all the better able to do for his change to the position of an outsider."—*Glasgow Herald.*

"It contains some of the best clerical stories—though not always of the most dignified nature, nor such as will tend to exalt the cloth in the estimation of rude and irreverent laics—that we have come across, and it gives very interesting, and for the most part accurate, details of the everyday life of the people."—*Elgin Courant and Courier.*

UNIFORM WITH "BENDERLOCH."

LOCH CRERAN. Notes from the West Highlands. By W. ANDERSON SMITH. Crown 8vo, cloth, 6s. Post free.

"Readers of Mr. W. Anderson Smith's *Benderloch* will welcome from the same pen a second instalment of notes of natural history in the Western Highlands entitled *Loch Creran.* . . . The influences of free moorland air and buoyant water, of a spacious heaven and wide horizon, are with us, and give zest to the study of fish and fowl and flower that are liberally displayed. Whether it is the flight of a solitary bunting, or the habitat of the pipe-fish (*Sygnathus*), the progress of *Mya* in the refluent tide or a nested robin domiciled among strange perils, the scenic suggestion cannot fail to persuade the senses. A large and distinctive portion of Mr. Smith's book is devoted to the investigation of the rich spoil of the dredger, as might be anticipated of so enthusiastic a student of fish culture, and many of the most interesting pages describe excursions on the waters of Etive and Creran and Benderloch, or among the rocky pools and stretches of sand exposed by the ebbing sea. By sea or land, on the wild hills or among the flowers and insects of his garden, Mr. Smith has ever something to say that is worth hearing, and he says it with admirable clearness and force."—*Saturday Review.*

"These charming notes from the Western Highlands are truly fascinating. Entering into the very spirit of the life and scenery by which he is surrounded, Mr. Smith gives his readers the benefit of the vast and out-of-the-way stores of information he has gathered in all branches of natural history. Each month, as it passes, has a chapter devoted to all its manifold changes and doings, and we get many glimpses of charming excursions, not unmixed with danger, when overtaken by those sudden climatic changes to which that grand wild mountainous coast is often exposed. An enthusiastic naturalist, the writer does not ride his hobby to death, but, like a true lover of Nature, his sketches are bright and fresh, and full of vivid descriptions, interspersed with many curious anecdotes and facts relating to both the animal and vegetable kingdoms. No better or more instructive guide to the fauna and flora of the Western Highlands could be had than Mr. Anderson Smith's most pleasant book."—*Literary World.*

"They will be well rewarded who follow Mr. Anderson Smith along the seashore, the hill-side, or the trouting stream; they will find how much a quiet and attentive eye can glean from a loving study of the denizens of earth, air, and water. The book is provided with a good index, and those who have not leisure or patience to read it through at a sitting may dip where they please. Like Mr. Smith's dredge, they hardly ever fail to bring up something of interest."—*Scotsman.*

"Students of natural history who read *Benderloch*, by Mr. W. A. Smith, will give a cordial welcome to *Loch Creran*, another and even more attractive work by the same observant author. With the exception, perhaps, of Mr. Jefferson, no living naturalist is gifted with a more picturesque manner of depicting the habits of birds, beasts, and fishes than is Mr. Smith. . . . Then what a vast fund of entertaining instruction is gathered in these excursions; a royal road to natural history is laid down by Mr. Smith, and the student follows it leisurely, culling charming bits of zoological lore here and there. One never knows what a new day may bring forth when accompanying Mr. Smith on his rambles. . . . There is, indeed, no end to the curious things observed by Mr. Smith. He seems only to sleep at home, for, with his waterproof handy, he roams about all day in the open air, and comes home at night with a well-filled note-book. . . . The wealth of interesting matter in this delightful volume is, however, tempting us beyond our space, and we think we have collated enough to make all who love the country, its sights and sounds, and health-giving breezes read the work itself."—*Dundee Advertiser.*

"To those who are familiar with Mr. Anderson Smith's *Benderloch*, no introduction or recommendation will be necessary on behalf of his new book, *Loch Creran*. The work is, in fact, as the preface explains, simply a continuation of the natural history sketches of which *Benderloch* is composed. . . . With what a happy combination of vivacity and patience, insight and enthusiasm, Mr. Anderson Smith scans the open pages of that great tome of nature. . . . Treasure-trove of this kind, along with notes of a more strictly scientific character, is freely scattered through Mr. Anderson Smith's pages; and so it will have a charm for every reader with healthy natural tastes."—*Scottish Leader.*

"There are few books in the language more delightful than White's *Selborne*, and in Mr. W. Anderson Smith that earnest Hampshire naturalist has a distinguished successor. His most recent volume is worthy of the author of *Benderloch*, a book which, it may be hoped, is already familiar to our readers. . . . The variety of his researches on land and water prevent monotony. The author has much to tell, and he explains what he has seen and done without waste of words."—*Illustrated London News.*

"Mr. Anderson Smith's observations extend over 1881-2, and refer mainly to the natural history of the district, but he deals also with other aspects of Nature, and his book is well worth reading."—*Times.*

"There can be no hesitation in assuring lovers of Nature that in *Loch Creran* they will find a work after their own heart. . . . The charm of the volume before us is that it is not the hasty outcome of the bookmaker feverishly eager to piece together into a volume odds and ends of information. There is an air of leisureliness about *Loch Creran*. Month by month are given the results of two years' close intercourse with loch and sea, field and wood. The work is one to be enjoyed by those who share the writer's tastes and spirit, and not to be rushed by the heedless."—*Graphic.*

"Every page has its charm, something at once to instruct the mind and to tickle and amuse the fancy. It is not a book to be read through at one sitting, but one to dip into occasionally and to ruminate over in pleased contentment. Perhaps its worth will be best appreciated by those taking a holiday in the country, or, above all, at the seaside. And it will serve as a very efficient guide to persons beginning the study of natural history, directing them what and how to observe. Many a capital story he gives illustrating the remarkable intelligence of the lower animals. Some of these border upon the marvellous."—*Perthshire Constitutional and Journal.*

"*Chatty and discursive, rather than elaborate, the interest in 'Loch Creran' is well maintained throughout, and the book appeals to the general reader, by whom it will doubtless be perused with greater pleasure than a more highly scientific disquisition.*"—*Pall Mall Gazette.*

"*He is a charming companion. His descriptions are vivid and true to nature—whether he makes us shiver and feel glad of the shelter of the house, as he tells us of winter's storms and floods, or whether he fills our hearts with a longing for the freshness and gladness of spring as he notes the signs of its advent on the shores of Loch Creran.*"—*Glasgow Herald.*

OLD CHURCH LIFE IN SCOTLAND:

Lectures on Kirk-Session and Presbytery Records. Second Series.
By ANDREW EDGAR, D.D.   Demy 8vo, cloth, 7s. 6d.   Post free.

"Antiquaries may welcome the minister of Mauchline as an elder brother of their craft. We have not seen the first series of lectures, but certainly these contain much that is queer and quaint. Odd people, these Scotch folks; but there is a homeliness and a reverence about them which we greatly value. Our author is evidently of the Established Church, and knows most about the old customs of that body, of which he writes with a twinkle in his eye which causes our eye to twinkle also. The grim want of humour in some of the proceedings is about the same thing as the presence of humour: you may laugh till you cry, and cry till you laugh; between the tremendously solemn and the ridiculous there is but a step. We have been so interested with the lectures that we must get the former volume. What times those must have been when guests at a funeral began to meet at ten in the morning, though the body might not be moved till three or four! Five or six hours! How did they spin them out? No marvel that the Kirk-Session had to hear charges of drunkenness. Such books as these are the best of history, leading us indeed into byways and lone paths which the general historian never traces."—**C. H. Spurgeon.**

MY COLLEGE DAYS: *The Autobiography*

of an Old Student. Edited by R. MENZIES FERGUSSON, M.A., Author of "Rambles in the Far North," &c.   8vo, cloth, 5s. Post free.

"Mr. Fergusson, either as author or as editor, has well earned our gratitude by giving us a volume which all may read with enjoyment and pleasure. . . . Space and its limits will not allow us to dwell on many other points of interest to be found in this entertaining volume; but we cannot pass without mentioning the worthy dame who said, in praise of her preacher: 'There's ae thing aboot yon man—he's a grand roarer.' Nor must we forget the careful landlady who was always anxious to know if her student-lodger was as yet an unengaged man, or, to use her own graphic phrase, was 'a bund sack set by.' . . ."—*Literary World.*

"We own to a suspicion that in this instance Mr. Fergusson has been his own literary executor. Whether this be the case or not, he has no reason to be ashamed of the bequest. The sketches have a pleasant grace of literary style, and a good deal of power in description of character-sketching, while there is in the writer a subtle under-strain of pawky humour, and he has brought together and put permanently on record a number of traditions of University life in Edinburgh and St. Andrews that are well worth preservation. . . . Our old student's reminiscences of St. Andrews, where he took the theological course after graduating in arts at Edinburgh, are not less lively or interesting than those he sets down respecting his Alma Mater; and his book is likely to take a place both on the shelves and in the enduring regard of many readers who have had similar experiences and tasted similar pleasures. A word of praise is due to the excellence of its typography and get-up."—*Scottish Leader.*

"We think the verdict will be that Mr. Fergusson has done well in publishing this thoughtful book. It abounds in vigorous, and, in many cases, eloquent delineations of University life; it is sympathetic in its spirit and catholic in its tone, especially when dealing with such subjects as the stage, so frequently abused. Its author was a student of the Universities of Edinburgh, St. Andrews, and Oxford, his reminiscences of which are often humorous, and always interesting. Some of the anecdotes recorded in this volume regarding the Edinburgh Professors are exceedingly entertaining. . . . We venture to predict for this autobiography a wide circulation."—*Dundee Advertiser.*

"The book is eminently readable, very quiet for the most part, but not without a few touches of gaiety and sprightly humour; and it betokens no little culture together with a strong poetic tendency. The contents are almost entirely confined to sketches of life at Scottish Universities, with some playful personal satire, of which various Professors, some mentioned by name and others denoted by initials, are the objects in chief, although the peculiarities of certain landladies whose province it is, or was, to let lodgings to students at Edinburgh or elsewhere, come in for their share of more or less satirical delineation. But there is nothing spiteful, nothing bitter, nothing cynical in the mode of treatment. Two chapters are devoted to a sketch, brief but graphic and sympathetic, of academic Oxford, whither the author went to sojourn and to study for two months."—*Illustrated London News.*

"This is a delightful book, calculated to afford much pleasurable amusement of a quiet kind. It is written in a light sparkling style. . . . The book itself is an enjoyable one, and perhaps none will read it with greater relish than the old fogies who see in it much of what they themselves passed through, and who, by the perusal, are led to recal, with mingled feelings, the aspirations, the freshness, and the frolic of their own College days."—*Perthshire Constitutional.*

"By those who have passed through the Universities it will be read with considerable pleasure, affording as it does such happy reminiscences of 'College days,' with their grave, plodding seriousness, or that more boisterous playfulness which is supposed to be the characteristic of students as a class. Those, again, who are simply outsiders, and have had no College days whatever, will be charmed by the recital here given of the doings of the students, and the customs associated with the respective Universities, the pen-portraits of the several professors, the opinions expressed regarding men and things, the poetry, original and selected, and the hundred and one subjects here treated of by a man of observant nature possessing facility of expression, besides a keen sense and appreciation of the humorous. . . ."
—*Stirling Observer.*

"Many a 'varsity man, who has won his degree in the modest 'little city, worn and grey,' will welcome the appearance of Mr. R. M. Fergusson's *College Days.*

Redolent every page of it, of the class-room, and the wild Bohemianism of student life, and bristling with the 'classic' ditties which have so often made the halls of St. Salvator's resound, here is material for a mental revel in the past."—*Northern Chronicle.*

"This series of autobiographical notes deserve recognition, if only because the style is perfectly natural and perfectly good-natured. . . . The book contains several capital anecdotes and some excellent verse."—*London Figaro.*

"But after all the charm of the volume lies in the whole life of a student which is presented to us, for his joys and his troubles, his amusements and his hard reading, are here written of by one who has evidently experienced all. Scattered throughout these pages are numerous verses, some original, some well-known students' songs. The original verses are very good. . . ."—*Stirling Journal.*

"The volume contains some very excellent poems which are worthy of finding, and doubtless will find, a place as verses to future songs. There is not a chapter in the book which is not thoroughly entertaining."—*The Tribune.*

"The 'Old Student' has to speak of Scotch Universities, Edinburgh, to wit, and St. Andrews, while he gives some impressions, gained as an outsider, of Oxford. . . . There is much that is interesting and entertaining, some good stories, and generally a pleasant picture of a happy and busy life."—*Spectator.*

"The writer is always entertaining and kindly, is wise in season, and also *desipit in loco*, and tells some good stories—professors being naturally his chief subjects."—*Pall Mall Gazette.*

"It is, to say the least, eminently probable that Mr. Fergusson relates his own experiences in Edinburgh and St. Andrews. He does so in a sufficiently lively and 'freshman' style. . . . *My College Days* is, on the whole, as readable as any book of the kind that has recently been published."—*The Academy.*

"Mr. R. Menzies Fergusson paints life as he thinks he saw it as a young man at St. Andrews and Edinburgh, in *My College Days*. This 'autobiography of an old student' contains much interesting reminiscence, and Mr. Fergusson has perhaps not erred in introducing into his text specimens of the verse into which some of his Caledonian student contemporaries were in the habit of dropping occasionally. Mr. Fergusson's little book should find many a sympathetic reader among former *alumni* of the Scottish Universities, for he writes without affectation.'—*Graphic.*

'Seldom have we had more pleasure than in the perusal of these reminiscences of College days. No one who has gone through the curriculum of a Scotch University can fail to attest the fidelity with which his experience here finds expression. . . . 'An Old Student' was privileged to have more than one *alma mater*. He could boast the fostering care of Edinburgh, of St. Andrews, and of Oxford, and of all these he has most pleasant reminiscences. Our author's experiences at Oxford will repay perusal. The whole book, written in a most happy, though thoughtful and affectionate strain, must incite the most cordial sympathy of all whose student days have not been forgotten, while the general public will peruse it with responsive hearts and a regretful feeling that they have missed the experiences of which it treats.'—*Brechin Advertiser.*

'The minister of Logie, who made a decided hit with *Rambles in the Far North*, has attempted a very difficult bit of work in *My College Days*. This purports to be the MS. legacy of a College friend who died young after some experience of student life in Edinburgh, St. Andrews, and Oxford. The fiction will impose upon nobody, although it may shield the editor from some blame, for while there is mirth and vigour and kindly reminiscence, there is also some very sharp criticism, and much reference to Academic dignitaries who are still in the flesh, and may be sensitive and inclined to sting when they find some of their class jokes not merely in print but bound in a book. . . . If certain Edinburgh divines beguile a leisure hour over these pages, they will for once see themselves as the keen-witted see them, and be amazed at the impudence of the rising generation. Everybody who knows Edinburgh will recognise the portrait of the preacher who is likened to Dr. Andrew Thomson in one thing—'There's ae thing about yon man, he's a grand roarer.' The St. Andrews part is full and cleverly done, and will have a charm for most *alumni* of the 'College of the scarlet gown,' because it contains a large number of the songs, original and selected, with which the lobby of the Natural Philosophy class-room was wont to resound."—*Elgin Courant.*

"The style is lively, and the descriptions of scenes of student life are graphic. The account of the election of Rector at Edinburgh will doubtless interest many, and the chapter dealing with landladies, their varieties and idiosyncracies, is humorous."—*Morning Post.*

"To recent students of our two greatest Scottish Universities—Edinburgh and St. Andrews—*My College Days* is charged with intense interest, though its racy humour and chatty discursiveness will render it attractive reading to those uninitiated in academic mysteries and innocent of student frivolities. The life of an Edinburgh student, in college and out of college, in the classroom, the debating society, the theatre, and the church, is described with untiring vivacity. . . . Whether author or merely editor, Mr. Menzies Fergusson is to be sincerely congratulated upon his success. Reminiscence is a species of literature not always instructive, not always even entertaining; in Mr. Fergusson's hands it becomes both."—*Fifeshire Journal.*

"We think the verdict of every impartial reader will be that Mr. Fergusson has done well in publishing this book. It abounds in vigorous, and, in many instances, impressive descriptions of University life; it is enlivened at judicious intervals with original verses, which evince lyrical power; its style is admirably condensed and clear; it is sympathetic in its spirit and catholic in its tone, especially when dealing with such subjects as the stage and its modern exponents by narrow-minded writers so frequently abused."—*Ayr Observer.*

"It is pleasantly written, is full of the fun of student life, full, too, of its hardships, abounds with excellent stories, is very discriminating in professional criticism, while scattered throughout the racy pages are many snatches of jovial college songs recorded nowhere else. . . . Altogether the volume is very readable, and no student, at all events, can find a dull page in it."—*Kelso Chronicle.*

THE TRAGEDY OF GOWRIE HOUSE.
An Historical Study. By LOUIS A. BARBÉ. Fcap. 4to, 6s.

In this new work on the interesting and mysterious episode of Scottish History, usually known as the Gowrie Conspiracy, the author has not only submitted the old materials to a close examination, but also thrown new light on the subject by the help of letters to be found in the Record Office, but overlooked or suppressed by former historians, of documents recently discovered by the Commission on Historical MSS., and also of important papers preserved in the French Archives.

"*A treasure of almost priceless thought and criticism.*"—*Contemporary Review.*

In the Press. Second Edition, Thoroughly Revised. Cr. 8vo, 333 pp., 7s. 6d.

WIT, WISDOM, AND PATHOS,

FROM THE PROSE OF

HEINRICH HEINE.

WITH A FEW PIECES FROM THE "BOOK OF SONGS."

SELECTED AND TRANSLATED BY

J. SNODGRASS.

"Mr. Snodgrass has produced a book in which lazy people will find a great deal to please them. They can take it up at any moment, and open it on any page with the certainty of finding some bright epigram; they need not turn down the page on shutting up the volume, as it matters little where they resume. There is nothing jarring in the whole book."—*Athenæum, April* 19, 1877.

"No Englishman of culture who is unacquainted with Heine can fail to derive a new intellectual pleasure from Mr. Snodgrass's pages."—*Contemporary Review, September* 1880.

"Mr. Snodgrass would appear to have saturated himself with Heine literature, to have so caught Heine's mode of thought and his turns of expression—quaint, droll, swift, and scathing by turns—that the translator would appear to have had no more difficulty in presenting Heine as he was to the reader than he would have in presenting his own thoughts." *Glasgow Herald, March* 31, 1879.

"Mr. Snodgrass, in his 'Wit,' &c., has done a great service in this respect, presenting as it were a full-length miniature of the man, clear and effective, wherein his characteristic expression is faithfully caught, and where, if we look carefully, we can see him as he really was, for he is made to paint his own portrait."—*British Quarterly Review, October* 1881.

"Mr. Snodgrass has certainly done great service to English literature in presenting us with a compact little volume like that before us."—*Spectator.*

"A word of cordial praise is due to the translator, Mr. J. Snodgrass, for his admirable performance of a very difficult task. His book is one to welcome and to keep as a treasure of almost priceless thought and criticism."—*Contemporary Review, February* 1881.

"Mr. Snodgrass is to be thanked for a very seasonable bit of work."—*Examiner, April* 26, 1879.

"We are bound to say that Mr. Snodgrass has done his work exceptionally well."—*The Literary World, May* 9, 1879.

"Mr. Snodgrass has made a valuable addition to English literature in this volume, and has given us a most attractive and efficient introduction to the study of Heine."—*The Nonconformist, August* 20, 1879.

"He has performed his task with skill, tact, and judgment; and it is easy to perceive that he has a thorough acquaintance with his author and sympathy for his matter."—*Notes and Queries, April* 19, 1879.

"The result of Mr. Snodgrass's attempt has been the production of a volume which, for variety and interest, may be pronounced one of the most successful books of the season."—*Aberdeen Journal, March* 26, 1879.

"In Heine, whose prose writings in German fill well on to a score of volumes, we find in remarkable combination the best qualities of German thought, along with the sparkle and brilliancy of an accomplished Frenchman's style."—*Aberdeen Daily Free Press, April* 21, 1879.

"Mr. Snodgrass has done his selection and translation admirably well, and we owe him thanks for a volume which has in it more wit of the highest sort, and more political insight, than any book that has lately been given to the public."—*Vanity Fair, November* 8, 1879.

"The compiler of this interesting little volume, Mr. J. Snodgrass, is perfectly right in saying that Heine is chiefly known to English readers as the author of the 'Book of Songs.'"—*The Week, April* 10, 1879.

"The 'English Fragments' have a special interest for the English reader; but the selection from Heine's prose works in general, most judiciously made and excellently translated by Mr. Snodgrass, gives a much completer view of the qualities of the writer's mind."—*Saturday Review.*

"Mr. Snodgrass has not essayed to give at all an exhaustive collection of Heine's witty, wise, and pathetic sayings; but he has selected, in the order in which they occur in the complete German edition, such extracts as have specially commended themselves to himself. He has produced a very enjoyable volume, exactly adapted to the taste of lazy and luxurious persons, who can just take up the book for five minutes to read a delightful passage, complete in itself, and not long enough to fatigue the most fastidious attention."—*Academy, May* 31, 1879.

ALEX. GARDNER, PAISLEY AND LONDON.

www.ingramcontent.com/pod-product-compliance
Lightning Source LLC
Chambersburg PA
CBHW031818220426
43662CB00007B/703